A NARRATIVE

OF THE

LIFE AND ADVENTURES

OF

WILLIAM BROWN,

NOW SCHOOLMASTER AT MIDDLEHAM, YORKSHIRE,

Who was

Thirteen Years

ON BOARD OF HIS MAJESTY'S SHIPS,

GLORY, BARFLEUR, TRIUMPH, ZEALOUS, GANGES, LIVELY, STAG, SPARTAN, &c.

INCLUDING

PRACTICAL OBSERVATIONS IN

VARIOUS PARTS ABROAD,

AND IN MOST PARTS OF ENGLAND;

AS, LONDON, MANCHESTER, SHEFFIELD, NOTTINGHAM, PORTSMOUTH, PLYMOUTH, LIVERPOOL, &c.

ALSO,

His Experience in Divine Things; a serious Address to Christians; a Word to Backsliders, &c.

THE WHOLE DESIGNED TO AMUSE AND INSTRUCT.

"*What pleasure had ye in those things whereof ye are now ashamed.*" ST. PAUL.

YORK:

PRINTED FOR THE AUTHOR,
BY T. WEIGHTMAN, 64, LOW-PETERGATE.
Price 2s. stitched.—2s. 6d. bds.

1829.

Entered at Stationers' Hall.

PREFACE.

Various are the motives that have induced men in all ages to write and commit the produce of their several pens to the press. It would be a very difficult task to determine, whether the motives urged in laborious essays, &c. are genuine or not; that a portion of them are so, there can be no doubt. If, for instance, a man writes and publishes on any subject, whether by way of Biography, History, Arts and Sciences, or any other branch of Literature, it is probable, that much egotism may be observable in his productions, or profit may be the prevailing principle—whereas, on the other hand, if a writer so far from extolling himself, opens out scenes which cause a blush at the remembrance of them, it may fairly be inferred his intention must be to guard others against the fatal rocks upon which he has split; and, to point out an antidote, must be a work worthy the reception of every candid reader. Such are the motives, and such the intention, of the present work; if an end so desirable to every one who feels for his fellow men as he ought, and which pious feeling is inculcated in our common Christianity, be answered in the smallest degree, I shall consider myself amply repaid.

WILLIAM BROWN.

A NARRATIVE

OF THE

LIFE AND ADVENTURES

OF

William Brown.

I was born at Thorverton, in Devonshire, on the 28th day of February, 1782, my father was by trade a Cooper, I had, when there, four brothers and a sister, my parents have had eleven children, six of whom are still living.

When I was only three months old my parents left Devonshire for London; leaving me and my brother John in the care of a grandmother. My parents were industrious, frugal, and strictly honest; and were, what the religious world are pleased to call, good moral characters; strictly adhering to the principles and doctrines of the established Church; but here I must observe, though I would willingly cast the mantle of love over a parent's nakedness, particularly so, as he has left the stage of mortality; yet I pledge myself to candour, and therefore must glance at his imperfections, as well as publish my own. The greatest evils I ever witnessed in him were, (after my arriving in London,) he would sometimes utter an oath, and I have known him, though not frequently, overcharged with liquor, his employment in a brewhouse might partially excuse the latter, but as he died in the true faith of the Gospel, and exulting in the sure and certain hope of a joyful resurrection, I now leave him, and return more immediately to myself.

My brother and me were sent to school when I was about three years of age, he being a year and a half older than me, but it is not my intention to fill up pages with mere frivolous nonsense, as nothing worthy of note transpired until I was six years old. I was then, with my brother, ordered to Exeter, and from thence we were conveyed to London ; on our arrival at the metropolis, I was struck, and somewhat alarmed, not so much at the magnificent structures, crowded streets, and spacious squares, as, I was at the motley group of chimney-sweeps which every now and then presented themselves to my view, adorned with gilt paper, having a shovel in one hand, and a brush in the other, it was their annual festival, and they danced what is commonly called the chimney-sweepers' jig, the shovel and brush were there only musical accompaniments; this jig, I soon got hold of, and never danced any other to this day.

On the propriety of employing our unfortunate fellow creatures in so disgusting an avocation, I do not feel it my duty to animadvert, so much having been recently argued in the public prints on the subject, but should there be urgent necessity for their continuance, it becomes the duty of others to sympathize with, and by every means in their power, to ameliorate their condition. I remember my mother's most effectual manner of commanding my obedience, was, by threatening to send me for a sweep.

Shortly after my arrival in town, I was sent to a day-school, and by associating with lewd boys, I imbibed their spirit and practices; the first discovery of my juvenile malpractices, was, my observing, when ordered to school, a six-pence which my mother had left on the mantel-piece, and though my parents had not, like too many, been in the habit of giving their children halfpence, to purchase fruit, sweetmeats, and toys, yet I knew what money was, I took the piece of silver unperceived, and on my way to school, purchased six pennyworth of oranges; on my arrival at school, the master enquired where I got money to make such a purchase, and on my telling him the truth, he sent them to my parents, who gave me a severe beating, and I promised to do so no more; shortly after this, I contrived another method of fraud, which was to bury the little sums, (which my mother entrusted me with, to fetch any articles of grocery,) under ground, between our house and the shop keeper's, and then obtained the articles on credit, this very often caused much ill-will between my mother and the creditor; my mother asserting she gave me money to pay with, and I as roundly persisting I had paid. When about eight Years of age, I was sent to Cripplegate School, for my father was frequently attacked with gout and rheumatism, which disorder carried him off nine years after; It was about this period that the dreadful fire broke out at Shadwell, at a sugar baker's, which lasted several days; one day on coming out of school in the afternoon, the whole atmosphere was illumined with the conflagration, and arriving at the spot a week after, the earth had contracted such intense heat, that I could scarcely stand on my feet.

At twelve years old, on a Thursday, having wrote badly, my master Mr. Peter Barry ordered me to remain in school at noon, on the afternoon of which day the boys have holiday, about two o'clock, Mr. B. came in and dismissed me; getting out of school I saw a break, (or vehicle in which they learn young coach horses to draw,) fancying I should sooner be at home I jumped up behind, the coachman beckoning me to come further forward, I got to the fore-part of the axletree, and in a minute or two found the coach was turning up Mr. Langhorn's yard, in Barbican, to whom it belonged, fearing a whipping for venturing so far, I attempted to get down, in doing which I got the two fore fingers of my right hand crushed to pieces, I then hastened home, roaring most tremendously, on arriving, my eldest brother was dispatched with me to Saint Bartholomew's Hospital, I remained there about nineteen weeks; the small remains of my fingers being healed, I was discharged; but I will mention an instance which occurred while at the Hospital, my arm being then in a sling. I contrived one day to evade the vigilance of my watchers, there being a sister and about four nurses to each ward, on getting into Little Britain I saw a number of boys playing at pitch halfpenny, on observing one of them pick up a six-pence, with a threatening aspect I addressed him as follows, "Come, sir, lay that six-pence down;" he replied, "Is it yours?" "You know that" said I, "and I have a good mind to give you a black eye and a bloody nose", on which he threw it down, and I immediately picked it up; there was a great demand at that time for cats' skins, and most boys wore caps made of them, on putting the six-pence in my pocket I walked a few yards, when my eyes were attracted by a cat standing at a pork butcher's door, I caught her tail with my left hand and swung her head under a cart's wheel which happened to be passing by, with this prize I ran to where I got the six-pence, and with one hand and a knife succeeded in skinning her, I then carried the skin to Cat-Gut Alley, Turnmill-Street, and there sold it for five-pence: having eleven-pence in possession, I repaired to the Hospital, on the upper story of one wing of which are two wards for the venereal, namely, Job and Lazarus, I found the men playing at what they called pitch at the bob, I challenged them one after another until I had completely drained them of all their Money, I had half a hat full of copper at least, the men were so enraged on my leaving them, that they threw shoes, hats, &c., at me; it was singular I should be so successful, being from circumstances mentioned, obliged to pitch with my left hand.

My next business was to appease the anger of the

sister of the ward I belonged to, this was easily effected; as I was aware she loved a drop of jackey, (gin) I procured a bottle, put some gin in it, and placing it in my bosom, repaired to my quarters; on seeing me she flew into a violent heat, telling me I should be turned out the next meeting, &c., I just let her see the neck of the bottle; the storm was over, and behold their was a great calm! Does not this simple instance in some measure resemble some modern *instantaneous conversions?* I say some; for I have no doubt others are genuine, nay, verily I have seen and witnessed many, I therefore need no further witness: but of the former an instance occurred but a fortnight since in my presence, at a chapel belonging to a recently established community; the minster full of zeal, after preaching long and loud, commenced a prayer meeting, and being determined if posible to save some, he applied to a poor young female, asking her if she was happy? the woman, perhaps understanding his meaning, said in desponding accents *no*, on which he knelt by her side, and I am persuaded shouted as loud as Baal's worshippers possibly could have done, had their lungs been made of brass; in this labour of love several others afterwards assisted; at length wearied with exertion, he again asked are you happy? she hastily replied, *yes;* the pious few rejoiced, and she was desired to attend at chapel the following evening, but strange to tell, the next morning, she publicly declared, she felt disgusted at their proceedings, and in reality felt more of misery than happiness, occasioned by being kept on her knees so long. I hope the kind reader will pardon not only this, but every digression I may make from my own personal experience, for

> "Be an author e'er so wise and wary,
> He may in some particulars miscarry."

I make no comment upon the beneficial and laudable effects of that noble institution, St. Bartholomew's Hospital, as they are too generally known to need it.

Upon returning thanks (as is customary) for the benefit received, I was discharged, and sent back to the same school I had left; I had not the same command of the pen as formerly, indeed I thought being lame in my fingers a good apology for negligence, but my master soon gave me to understand that though I could not write so well as aforetime, yet I could write as well one day as another. I soon grew weary of school duty, and determined (in spite of the remonstrances of my parents) to leave, I did so at thirteen years of age, and not liking to stop at home, I went to live at a neighbouring house as pot boy, my employ was to carry out beer, fetch in the pots, &c.; It was but a short time before an incident occurred; I mention it because it was the first time I remember ever to have tasted ardent spirits (would it had been the last). I was setting skittles up in the skittle alley, and was sent by one of the playing party to fill a pint of porter; on getting into the cellar I observed the spirit safe or rack door open, which was generally kept locked, I took advantage of this, and drew my pint nearly full of gin, and drank it off, I then filled it with beer and went back to my work, in a few minutes my head began to swim, and I knocked the skittles down as fast as I set them up; my master became acquainted with it, took me by an ear and lugged me up stairs to bed, the next day he gave me a good strapping.

It is a common practice with publicans in London, to take an account of the quantity of beer the servants carry out in their trays, and the latter, upon returning, must account for the delivery; one day, when out, I fancied I had a pint overmuch, and a stranger wanting a pint I put the three pence in my pocket, but in giving in my accounts found out my error, a lie was instantly suggested, and I told my master that my mother had taken two pints instead of one, and going to the door I ran to my mother advising her to say the same, should any enquiry be made; my master made it his business to go to my mother immediately, (no doubt a little suspicious of me,) and on asking how many pints she had had, she replied two; fortunately an empty pint stood by the side of the Fire, and the full one on the table. Up to this time, from my coming to London, my parents had lived in the Parish of St. Luke's.

I was now arrived at my fourteenth year, and from that time, to the fifteenth, I lived at no less than from fifteen to twenty places as errand boy, pot boy, &c., in some of these I remained three days, in others a week, &c., I lived with a cheese monger in Holborn about three weeks, and having been out with butter, I purchased a pair of half boots and paid the money out of the price of the butter, it being due to me; upon my master scolding me on this account, I determined to vex my litigious mistress by telling her I was half starved in her service; I got a tub of water thrown over me and so ended this service.

Being one evening short of money, I hit upon a project to get some; the ballad singers of London were at that time singing with great eclat, the song called the Arethusa; I determined to take advantage of the circumstance, so getting a number of old newspapers, in the evening I took my station at the end of several streets, (having previously cut them into slips resembling songs) I began to sing the above, and so rapid was the sale, (in the dark) that in a quarter of an hour I had sold about forty at a halfpenny each, not considering it safe to remain too long in a place I shifted into the middle of Chancery-Lane, Holborn, where I struck up as usual; when I had sold about twenty more an old gentleman opened a door opposite to me, he had a wig on, held a candle in one hand and a stick in the other, and said to me "you scoundrel, if you dont get you gone directly I'll have you sent to the watch house;" I bade him good night and departed, I then went to live with a watch springer and liner, here I found great facility in making money, in this branch of business they make gold and silver shavings and dust from scooping out the cases, these are dropt into a drawer, separate from each other, so that if an errand boy is so disposed, he may help himself to either *in small proportions, frequently* without detection, and gold refiners and others are always ready to purchase what ever is brought to them from such young traders in iniquity; my master was partial to me, and had I discharged my duty faithfully would have learnt me his trade, but an unlucky circumstance drove me from his roof, being sent for some satin to line some cases, on my road I saw a number of boys surrounding a woman, she had a board with a tetotum, (as they called it) I determined to try my luck (but it was with my master's money,) I won the first time, when flushed with my success I tried again, but soon lost all to the amount of three shillings and six-pence, there was no alternative but to return without the satin, or obtain it upon credit.

I fixed upon the latter, my master soon found it out, and my father being informed of it, beat me most unmercifully; I would gladly have left out the following, but having pledged myself to reserve nothing material, I subjoin it; having attended to see two malefactors executed at Newgate, a pieman was bawling out, "toss or buy," "toss or buy," and having three halfpence on me, I lost it in tossing, the man put other three halfpence to it, requesting me to fetch him a pint of beer from the public house, immediately opposite to where he stood, I entered the front door and slipt out at the back, but saw no more of the pieman. I endeavoured to justify myself for this act, on the ground of the pieman's impropriety in selling and tossing for pies at an execution. Punishment, doubtless, of so awful and public a nature, is intended as a warning to others but it is certain it had no effect whatever on me.

As about this time I took my leave of the metropolis of England, may I not say of the world, the seat of every virtue and every vice; I beg leave to return to the time of my arriving at it, and, taking a cursory view, make such remarks as I proceed as may suggest themselves to me, intended for the mutual benefit of both masters and servants, also to point an antidote to prevent such nefarious practises. First, then, let the superb palaces, stately edifices, magnificent theatres, &c., remind my readers that the time is fast approaching when all these things shall be mouldered in the dust; when as Shakspeare expresses it— "The cloud capp'd towers, the solemn temples the gorgeous palaces, yea, the whole globe itself, and all which it inherits shall dissolve, and like the baseless fabric of a vision, leave not a wreck behind."

The next thing I would guard my readers against is, that of negligently laying their money on shelves, tables, &c. within the reach of those whose tender years cannot discern between good and evil, purloining the sixpence, mentioned in the early part of this work, was the first improper act with which I can charge myself, and I am not certain the impression made on my mind by the buying the oranges with it, did not create in me a longing for money.

Again, the too common practice of parents indulging their children to excess, particularly in giving them money to spend, cannot be too cautiously guarded against, the evil is twofold, first it injures the parents more seriously in their money concerns than they are aware of, remember one farthing per day amounts to seven shillings and seven-pence farthing per year. It would be well did none exceed this, if parents would train up children in the way they should go, teach them the lesson so forcibly urged upon us by St. Paul; "Having food and raiment, let us be therewith, content." if parents once begin this evil, no one knows where it will end, for of children it may be said as of parents in general, much would have more and more would have all, if once indulged they will expect a continuance of the same with increase. I have said more than I intended on this head; being myself a teacher of youth. The general and incalculable utility of charity schools,—Sunday schools, &c., is universably admitted I would observe (however preposterous and full of incongruity it may appear) that I felt a love which I could not account for to the Bible, and to preaching, during the last year I spent in London, but I confess I knew nothing of the import or meaning of the one or the other. I think it was in the year 1798, I first had an offer of going to Sheffield, in Yorkshire, as an apprentice to a pawnbroker, which I accepted, my parents attended me to the Bull and Mouth Inn, Bull and Mouth Street, London, we parted affectionately and the evening following I arrived safe at Mr. Peech's Angel Inn, Sheffield, from thence I was conducted to my after residence, I was perhaps two months with Mr. M. previous to being bound, my master was a widower of about forty, having four children, three sons and a daughter, he had in connexion with a Mr. B. of Nottingham four shops at Sheffield, one at Rotherham, one at Derby, and one in London, business was very brisk and Mr. B. being the most assiduous man in business I ever remember to have met with, promised to realize an independence in a short time. He was a member of the Methodist Society, and was an example worthy of imitation for his strict attention to family worship, his regular attendance at the means of Grace, and his studious endeavours to bring not only his children but his servants also to a sense of their duty to God and man; it has often been a matter of dispute among religionists, whether the carrying on the business of a pawnbroker, is consistent with or repugnant to scripture, I am aware under the mosaic or jewish dispensation, the practice is prohibited by several plain passages, but whether those passages are still binding I leave to those who make them a bone of contention. If I recollect right a meeting was convened and my master turned out, not being willing to relinquish so lucrative a profession; in order to make a right estimate or to ascertain whether upon the whole it be beneficial or injurious to society, we must weigh both sides impartially.

First, its advantages; I have known many shopkeepers and other very respectable persons, who could not make up a payment, when such payment became due, in cases of this kind, I have known as much as one hundred pounds, advanced on property which has often been redeemed in a few days, by which means the credit of the tradesman has been kept up, by paying short of two and a half per cent, ticket money included, (I mean for any time within the month,) it must be admitted, this is an accommodation,—other instances of travellers, &c., might be adduced, whose finances have been exhausted, by leaving in pledge a watch or other articles they have thereby been enabled to pursue their journey; I say that these are conveniences none can reasonably be disposed to deny. Added to this the very serious sum the pawnbrokers pay to the revenue yearly, these considerations argue in favor of them.

Secondly, the disadvantages; and probably these are principally confined to the working classes and the poor, they too frequently habituate themselves to this kind of traffic, which proves very detrimental, I have known scores who have regularly pawned their sunday clothes, bible, &c. every Monday morning, and redeemed them as regularly every Saturday, thereby paying four times as much as the law allows, the interest of a day or week being charged the same as a month.

Again, if a person is disposed to recreation tipling or what not, he knows he has but to pay his *uncle* a visit, make a deposit and he may satiate his propensity, perhaps to the hurt of a wife and family, having glanced at both sides of the question, I beg leave to dismiss the subject, leaving the points proposed to the decision of a disinterested and an unbiassed public.

A singular circumstance and one which demands our sympathy, has just occurred to my mind, a poor woman in her need, pawned her gown, petticoat, and stays at our shop, for fifteen pence, and for fourteen years successively payed the interest amounting to two guineas, besides ticket money, but unfortunately for her she could pay the interest no longer, and she had the mortification to see her clothes exposed for public sale. It was an expression of Mr. B's, "where I am, (meaning where he attended divine service,) there shall my servants be also," and this was punctually attended to by all the domestics, he regularly sat under the methodist ministry in Norfolk-street, and garden walk chapels, Miss Mary Barrett, (now Mrs. Taft) visited Sheffield, this pious woman both from report and observation had been an instrument of much good by her unwearied labours in the ministry, I had previous to her coming attended preaching a few times, and began to feel a spirit of enquiry respecting the christian system. she had breakfasted one sunday morning at our house, and it being chapel time, Mr. M. and Mrs. T. set off for chapel, I took this opportunity of running to our garden, and cramming my pockets full of apples ran as fast as I could to chapel, Mrs. T. was in the pulpit, and our seat was in the bottom just before her; while she prayed I heard her exclaim, "away with such a religion as will not keep us honest," I observed her pointing to me, I looked at my coat pockets when a large rosy cheek'd apple stood full in view, in my haste to crush it down, I forced three or four out which made a terrible rumbling on the boarded floor, I thought all was over, that she certainly knew all about it, and that she would tell my master. I waited impatiently the conclusion of the service, and ran first out, throwing all my illgotten fruit into the first privy I came to; but never heard about them after; how true is the saying, "the wicked flee when no one pursueth, and fear where no fear is."

Allow me to mention the following, though calculated merely to excite a smile; my fellow apprentice, myself and another young man, rose early one morning to get some clover for our rabbits, taking with us a pair of shears, and a brace of pocket pistols charged with powder, also a sack to put the clover in, we had sheared a nice corner of a field, when a country fellow came towards us vociferating oaths and curses, I had one of the pistols, I called to him, and told him if he advanced a yard nearer, I would certainly shoot him, pointing the piece at him, (it was small and I believe he did not perceive it,) "Dam thee, thee shoot," "thee shoot" he exclaimed, I fired, "now Jack" said I "shoot him dead," "I will by heav'n" said he, he presented his pistol, upon seeing which the fellow bawled out "murder, murder, murder," with all his might, then took to his heels jumping over hedges, ditches, gates, and every thing that came in his way, we got off safe with our booty. A few mornings after the same party set off to get a stick each, while we were cutting some young trees, at the back of the barracks, we were suddenly surrounded by a party of soldiers, they seized two of us, the other escaped, we were escorted into the barrack yard, while the corporal was gone, as I suppose to make the complaint, I ran to the bottom of the yard and dropped down a wall at least five yards high unhurt, my comrade followed, we were closely pursued, but the river running the opposite side of the road, we both took the water swam over and made our escape. I now began to feel a relish for the theatre, although we never could go with Mr. M's leave, yet there being four of us in the shop we made a practice to let one another in after the family were in bed, and if the question was asked "where is William," the answer invariably was "*in bed sir*," we never could get but at half price.

My young master had lain for several days bad of a fever, on my going into his room to see him, he told me he could eat a bird if I could shoot him one, I had never fired a gun in my life, however I went into the warehouse got a gun and loaded it, putting three pipes full of shot in, I fired from my bed room window, at a bird perched on a wall at the bottom of the yard, the shock nearly stunned me, dreading my master's hearing the report, I threw the gun under the bed and ran down into the shop but no notice had been taken of it; the wall went with a great descent and a row of houses being opposite, I made no allowence for the descent; I was left by myself in the shop and in a few minutes in came an old woman, she had seen many ups and downs in the world, one leg being much longer than the other. "Where" said she, "where is the villain that wanted to take my life, what harm did I ever do you? oh, its you—I see" said the woman. I was much alarmed and began to explain when a man entered and said he had just past the woman's door, heard the report of a musket and a crash of glass, on turning back he found seven squares of glass broken, the door full of shot, and the old lady nearly in a fainting fit, with her pipe broke in her hand; I begged the old dame to be off, promising to repair damages, which I did.

I now got acquainted with some church singers and joined them to sing at the parish church, from that time I have been a lover of harmony;—we had also a catch and glee club, and met once a week, at a public house, in Scotland-street, where a hot supper was provided at the expence of several gentlemen; my several engagements made me less attentive and less anxious to please my employer than before, my master kept a horse and gig, I and a younger apprentice used to clean the horse each night alternately, on Mr. M's returning home one evening, he ordered me to clean the horse, I growled and said it was John's turn, upon which he told me had he ordered John to have done it he should have done it—" what I order to have done, I'll have done ;' upon which I banged the door too went into the stable and taking up the fork, began to beat the dumb animal; Mr. M. had followed me and was peeping in at the door, " I see you; I see you, William," said he, " these things will never do you any good,"—how often have I felt the force of those words since. Our confinement was close in the shop, and if Mr. M. knew it, would never suffer us to take a walk after the shop was shut up—his motive doubtless was good, but we could not relish it. One evening John and I determined to take a walk, we were no more than twenty minutes absent, we found however all the family were gone to bed, except the Housekeeper, on our asking what was for supper, she said, " Master had taken the keys of the cupboard." "Well, John" said I, " let us go and forage," we examined some time and found an excellent tea cake, sent from lawyer B's lady to Mrs. M. (I had forgot to mention my master's recent second marriage to a Miss B. of Grimesthorpe). I thrust my hand down the middle of it, John did the same; now said John, I'll pull if you'll pull—we divided it, eat the cake, and retired to rest. Early next morning the cake was missing, we were both called into the parlour and acknowledged eating it, upon which Mr. M. took his whip, and after thrashing John, turned to commence operations upon me, on which I seized the whip and thrust it into the fire, Mr. M. was dreadfully alarmed, and staggering backward, cried aloud for assistance, telling me if I struck him he would send for a constable; I told him I knew better than to strike him, neither would I be struck by any man in England.

It will be recollected by my readers, in the year 1801 or 2,—every article of provision was excessively dear, and the Magistrates recommended masters to give their servants herrings or eggs in lieu of meat. Mr. M. purchased a barrel of herrings, there were at this time three young men in the shop (including myself), the herrings were cooked and we marched from the shop to the kitchen; finding our dinner was a red-herring each, we opened them, the two other young men nailed theirs up in the kitchen, and I tied mine to the knocker of the door. The master coming, ordered us into the shop; going through the kitchen he cast his eyes upward, saw a herring nailed to a beam, and another over the fire place, tearing them down in a rage, he went into the yard, not observing mine, however upon his return, he had some corn in his hand, and was walking backwards, feeding some chickens, when feeling for the knocker he laid hold of my herring, he gave us a severe lecture, and said, we should have nothing else 'till they were eaten, but we saw no more of them. This induced me to write the following lines:—I give them verbatim as I wrote them at that time.

> In Sheffield town a man there lived,
> Near West Bar Green resided,
> Not far from Tom Smith's, the blue boar,
> Although contrary sided.
>
> A 'prentice boy he then must have
> From London town so sprightly,
> He was not long ere he got one,
> Which seemed to suit him tightly.
>
> A lawyer he was then sent for,
> To bind this lad so neatly,
> 'Till twenty three years old and turned,
> This did not go down sweetly.
>
> The deuce go with all those that bind
> A lad 'till three and twenty;
> The devil bind them by the ears,
> 'Till they've had binding plenty.

Four years of his apprenticeship
Being expired nearly;
He wanted to horsewhip me now
For which he paid most dearly.

A warrant for me then he got
To apprehend and seize me,
Before my betters to appear,
Good Lord, how this did teaze me!

"Says he, my servants live like kings
And want for no good thing;"
At which the Justice shook his head
Can you deny this thing.

Says I, if kings are forced to eat
Red herrings twice a week,
Without a doubt we live like kings,
If this is fat'ning keep.

Red herrings they are seldom seen
In any palace royal,
When any come into our house
We call them mackaroyal.

We kick them up and down the house,
They kick up such a stink;
The fire-back's sure not to lack,
We cram some down the sink.

was now in my twenty first year. One morning a decent looking middle aged man, accompanied by two females, entered our shop, (which afterwards proved to be his wife and daughter,) he wanted to purchase a riding habit for the fair young one, I endeavoured to accommodate them, particularly the daughter; she was well made, modest in her aspect, handsome in her features, and had a pair of eyes which seemed to be the seat of beauty and innocence, with the latter she gave me a glance which seemed to speak unutterable things. Prior to this I was a stranger to love, I confess I felt pleasingly comical; the father observed my perturbation, and requested my company to tea on the sunday following, at the light horseman public house, near the barrack; I readily accepted the invitation, and although this was on the Friday it seemed a month to the time. On sunday I went, drest in my best, and with an air of as much consequence as I could muster. The father, mother, and loveliest of daughters, received me in the most cordial and friendly manner. The father was master farrier in the Warwickshire Fencibles, and the regiment was about to be broke up, he informed me he had saved in the regiment about seven hundred pounds, and was at a loss to know what occupation to follow upon the regiment being disbanded, he said he had thoughts of the public line, and wished me to give my advice, whether that or the sale of new and second-hand wearing apparel would answer his purpose best; (we dealt in the latter to a very great extent), I recommended the sale business, convincing him at the same time, that my profits arising from the same during the last quarter of a year averaged eight pounds per week.

This was actually the case, but I was considered the best salesman in the shop, and was consequently set apart for that purpose; he immediately acquiesced with my views, and I promised to give him reference to the first wholesale dealers in London, with whom we traded to the amount of four or five thousand pounds per annum. It may seem a serious sum, but it must be recollected we had the other five shops to supply regularly: after tea, wine, &c., I was invited to take a walk by Miss R. you may imagine this was most grateful to my feelings, so we walked and talked about such things as nature dictated, indeed I would have been mute, would my companion have allowed it, but the exchange of words were mutual, I listened to the accents which fell from her ruby lips with rapture, her very eyes sparkled with intelligence, the notes of the sweetest warblers of the groves seemed harsh and discordant, and an unpardonable interruption to love's reverie.

"Of joys that are past, never to return again, how painful the remembrance," I had read the *Sorrows of Werter*, and spurned is weakness with indignation, considering myself proof against all the artillery which the fair sex could bring, after exchanging mutual vows of eternal friendship, the shades of evening coming on, we were obliged reluctantly to return homeward; at our parting she favoured me with a taste of those lips from which such honied words had fallen. I had in my conversation with Mr. R. informed him that I was not free from my apprenticeship 'till I was upwards of twenty three, he assured me that if I claimed my indenture on the day I was twenty one, my master could retain me no longer; fired with the thought, and at the same time of enjoying the object of my wish—I grew indifferent to my master, and on the slightest occasion would remind him I should soon be one and twenty, and would then leave him, Mr. R. took a shop within fifty yards of my master's, and I gave directions for fitting it up, which was done accordingly, and Mr. R. ordered clothes from London to furnish it, I went every opportunity to see my dear Miss R. and was always treated as one of the family. At length the long wished for day arrived, on the 28th of February, 1803, being twenty one years of age, I claimed my indenture; my master refused to deliver it up, he was going the next day on business to London, and this being Saturday (a very busy day with us) I took advantage of it, and immediately applied to Justice Wilkinson for a summons which was granted, I brought it to the constable and he served it immediately, under circumstances he was obliged to agree to board me at the Blue Boar until his return from London; he was absent three weeks and you may judge where I spent most of my time.—Mr. R's goods had arrived, and I was placing them in the shop, &c., all was remarkably pleasant in this family during the absence of Mr. M.; at length he returned and answered the summons, which was referred to the next Justice meeting and it was then and there determined that no indenture was legally binding after the age of twenty one. The case had been determined by taking the opinion of the twelve Judges upon a similar one, which was as follows;—A girl had been put out an apprentice by a parish in London at the age of seventeen, and bound for seven years, when she was twenty years old a cousin died leaving her upwards of seven hundred pounds, of course she was anxious to be released.

She was advised (as I was) to claim her indenture at twenty one, she did so, and the opinion of the judges was as above stated. My indenture was cancelled accordingly and I received it.

Elated with my present success, and more so by future prospects, I flew to the residence of Mr. R. told him to congratulate me on my good fortune, and shewed him my indenture; there was a marked coolness and indifference in his aspect, and after taking dinner, he told me that himself, Mrs. R. Miss, and a son Thomas were sufficient to carry on the undertaking, that my required salary could not be paid, and ultimately that I had better provide myself a better situation, thunderstruck, I stood scarcely believing my own ears, at length observing to my mortification that *Miss R.* by her looks and gestures sanctioned what had fallen from the lips of her perfidious father, " base man," said I, "is this the return for my kind attentions to your future welfare, and you Miss R. where are your solemn vows, where now your protestations of love and attachment, I leave you to your own reflections, if you have a reflecting mind; learn hence, that to raise confidence and then disappoint it, is one of the worst of crimes,—

farewell!"—I never spoke to any of them after. Being thus nonsuited, I went to a Mr. B. a pawnbroker, and told him of the treatment I had met with, he informed me I was welcome to remain with him until I could find a situation to my mind, I consented to do so. A few days after I went to the Blue Boar, a man came in and called for a pint of beer, he had a handkerchief containing (as it afterwards proved) silver watches, gold rings, and other articles of value, after drinking his pint he put his hand into his pocket and took out a considerable bundle of bank notes; Thomas S. the landlord was (and is still) constable; on observing the notes, he said to him, "Friend, you have been lucky." "yes," he replied, "I have been receiving a lot of prize money at York, pray," said he, " can you inform me where I can get lodgings."—he directed him to a lodging house in the neighbourhood. Early the next morning, the constable came to me and enquired if I observed the man the evening before at his house, I said, " yes;" he then shewed me a hand bill, offering a reward of twenty guineas for the apprehension of any person or persons who had committed a burglary on the premises of a Mrs. Booth, watchmaker and silversmith, Huddersfield, to be paid by the association for the prosecution of felons; the maker's name and number of the watches were on the hand bill. I told him I would take him; he answered, "I am afraid he is too far gone, as he left his lodgings at four o'clock this morning." Three mornings after I was cleaning Mr. B's shop windows outside, and observed the man coming towards me with the same handkerchief in his hand. On his passing me I said, " it was a fine morning ;" he replied, " yes ;" when he asked me if I wanted to buy a few watches, assuring me I should have them very cheap; I desired him to walk into the shop, I followed, and after ascertaining that they were the identical watches mentioned in the hand bill, I bargained with him for six at one pound ten shillings each; after fumbling in the till for some time, I told him I must fetch some more money, when on entering the parlour I told my master I had got the man who had robbed Mrs. B. he asked what I was about I told him making the above bargain, and desired he would come into the shop and say he wanted no watches, he did so, the man packed them up again and left the shop. " Zounds," said Mr. B. "you have let him go." "Oh," said I, " he is the safer for that," I followed, and on passing him, asked if he would have share of a pint of ale, he said he had no objection, I proposed to go to the Blue Boar; " no," said he, " any where but there." We were passing a skittle alley, and a number of men were playing, we went into the house and I called for a pot of ale; I had tipt a wink to an acquaintance of mine as I passed the players, he came and asked what I wanted, I told him to fetch Thomas Smith, he went but Mr. S. not being at home his assistant Jones came, after drinking with us, he asked me what I wanted, I said, take charge of this man; " what do you suspect," said he; I replied, "a burglary on the premises of Mrs. Booth of Huddersfield." " I charge your assistance in the King's name," said Jones. We took him down to Smith's and when he came home he was agreeably surprized to see the supposed object of his search locked to the bar of his grate; he then accosted the prisoner as follows: "friend wast thou ever at Huddersfield;" he said, "he did not know, he had been at so many places." Smith then opened the handkerchief and found most of the stolen property. There were among the rest the dozen gold rings. The man was taken before a magistrate and fully committed I was never called upon before the justice, which surprized me, as the hand bill stated whoever apprehends or causes to be, &c.; now in fact I had done both, I remonstrated with Mr. S. and he assured me it was of no consequence as I should be subpœnaed at York assizes; the assizes came on, the man was tried, found guilty, and sentence of death was recorded against him, I applied again to Mr. S. and after several evasions he told me I had no business with it whatever. I made no answer, but a few days after I rode to Huddersfield, and claimed the reward at Mr. Ingham's banking house. He pleaded pity on behalf of the widow acknowledged the right of my claim, said Mr. S. had applied, but to no purpose; I desired one of the clerks to bring me paper and ink, and I wrote to the following effect.

These are to certify that I William Brown, have received the sum of five guineas as a full compensation for the apprehension of Samuel Haggar, charged with a burglary on the premises of Mrs. Booth, of Huddersfield,—witness my hand, &c. &c.; they gave me the sum mentioned with hearty thanks, and an old gentleman present insisted on my receiving half a guinea from him, he being an intimate friend of Mrs. B's.

In a short time after my return to Sheffield, I had business at the justice room, T. S. came in, and asked me with a menacing look, whether I had been at Huddersfield, I said I had, how much money did you get, I wont tell you said I, he said I was a D— scoundrel and he would enter an action against me, I informed him, if he swore in court, I would certainly have him fined. I heard no more of this concern, but that the man was reprieved from death, and transported.

My present master Mr. B. had often been robbed by persons coming, looking at, and sometimes purchasing a trifling article and embezzling more valuable ones, to prevent or detect which I made a practice of counting any kind of article asked for by the dozen, I did this unperceived by the customer. One day a man came in, to purchase a gold ring, having counted twelve, I threw them carelessly on the counter, he purchased one, which cost us three and sixpence, paid for it and went away, observing there were but ten remaining, I followed asking him if he would have share of a pot of ale; he consented and we went to Mr. S's called for it and when Mr. S. brought it in, I told him to take charge of the man, as I suspected he had stolen a gold ring, the man fell on his knees, took the two rings out of his pocket, and implored forgiveness, I would gladly have done so, having recovered my master's property, but the constable was inexorable, the man was committed to

Wakefield House of Correction, and sentenced at the quarter sessions, to be imprisoned for three months.

I was now applied to by a Mr. B. a stone mason, who was about to commence business in our line. I agreed to conduct it for three years for a certain salary, to be augmented each successive year. I went to see my friends in London, while the shop was preparing. On my return my master took an apprentice to assist me; we agreed very well for the first year, but my mistress and the boy, had been prying into the business, and thought themselves competent to manage it; In fact they told me so, upon my reminding Mr. B. of our engagement, he laughed at me asking what writings I had to produce. It is true, we had no more than a verbal agreement, but my last master, Mr. B. was privy to it; I employed a Mr. T. solicitor, and the case was heard before a justice of the quorum, the point could not be cleared up and we had either to agree by arbitration, or carry it to the quarter sessions, we agreed to the former, and in consideration of Mr. B's paying a certain sum we separated.

As I am on the eve of leaving my narrative, so far as it relates to Sheffield, I wish to make some observations respecting my views of religion, during my residence at that place. My readers will remember my mentioning when a youngster, my attachment to the Bible, and the stated ordinances of God's house, in addition to this, I always had a presentiment that the Almighty, had intended me to preach the Gospel; where this persuasion came from I know not, this I know, from the moment I discovered in the smallest degree the spirituality of the divine law, observed its requirements, aw what man was in his natural state, his restoration by Christ, understood the nature of Gospel repentance, faith in the redeemer, justification, sanctification, and perfect holiness, I felt an ardent desire of knowing these things experimentally, and I felt such a strong attachment to any that appeared to have experienced the deep things of God, that I would have gone through fire and water for them.

I reflect with pleasing emotion at this moment on a Miss S——r, Miss U——n, Mrs. P——s, a departed saint L——n, L——k, Wm. H——y, and scores of others, some remaining to this day, some gone to their eternal reward. I cannot but feel gratitude to God for the pious exhortations of that eminent man of God, Henry Longden, what a solemn charge did he give me in his study in Broad Lane, to be careful not to forget to "stir up the gift of God that was in me." Oh, that his many prayers, &c., may not be finally lost upon me. I cannot pass over those faithful labourers in the word and doctrine; viz.:—Wood—Nelson—Pipe—Miller—Bramwell,—&c., under their ministration I have felt powerful awakenings, strong convictions, and made strong resolutions of amendment of life.

I would observe here that though I am avowedly against publishing dreams, yet the following I related to P. P. then a class leader at Sheffield, (and who I believe resides their still) on the morning after it happened. I dreamt I was on Ludgate Hill, London, leading to and commanding a view of St. Paul's Church-yard; I was struck with astonishment at beholding thousands of men and women assembled in the church-yard, a man observed to me, "you seem alarmed young man," I said, "pray, sir, what is the reason of that vast concourse of people meeting together." What said he, sternly, "don't you know. I answered in the negative, then said he, "awful is your case." He then directed my attention upward, and told me the day of Judgment was come; I perceived winged seraphs flying in every direction in the ____ saw the throne—I saw the books opened and the ____ sitting as described by Daniel—the seraphs appeared to have each a large bladder filled with wind. I asked the stranger what their commission was, he answered all that are to be damned will be struck with one of those bladders. I hastened homeward, but on entering Long Lane, West Smithfield, an angel struck me on the back with one of the bladders, uttering at the same instant, "thou art damned." I immediately fell down and endeavoured to pray, but could not; in a moment I found myself at my master's door at Sheffield, and had hold of the latch, when I received two heavy blows like the former, and a voice like thunder exclaimed again, "damned, damned." When I related this dream in the morning, P. P. enjoined me in the strongest terms to think seriously and turn to the Lord with full purpose of heart. The words of a pious widow—have followed me ever since, "unstable as water thou shalt not excel." She was well known at Sheffield, her name was Radford.

Much has been said on the subject of revivals, my Sheffield friends have had a large share of those glorious days, they have generally been when the circuit has been blest with men full of faith and of the Holy Ghost, men who counted not their lives dear unto them if by any means they might save souls from death. How has Norfolk Street Chapel rung with the praises of God when on every hand souls were crying for mercy, when the glory of God filled the place; who will not join with me as in years that are past, in singing " Haste again ye days of Grace." It was highly gratifying to me (low as I had fallen) after having been tost about on the ocean for near thirteen years, to see many who were the fruits of the great revival at Sheffield standing fast in the liberty wherewith Christ had made them free. I was invited into the singing seat by my old companion and friend James Frith, the leader of the singers, who succeeded John Wild. I was filled alternately with grief and joy—grief to see so many had taken their flight,—joy—at seeing a Wilkinson, a Miss Unwin, and several others, I trust fast ripening for an upper and a better world. I must now dismiss this pleasing part of my history and proceed.

Being out of employ, and my small stock of money exhausted, I pledged the best of my wearing apparel. I was then employed to do business in the Cutlery line at Manchester by commission, I got some good orders and resided at the latter place two or three months; at length the Theatre (that bane of godliness) again allured me, which led to every excess of riot; I sold my pattern card to a barber on Shude Hill, for half a guinea, sending my accounts home to my employers.

The next thing which attracted my attention was a handbill wanting recruiting serjeants, and although I knew no more about soldiering than the man in the moon, yet I thought I would see what I could make out; so accordingly I went to Lieutenant D. in Deansgate, and offered my services; he asked me if I was acquainted with the recruiting service, "Oh, yes," said I, "my father has been in it all his life time." This was a palpable falsehood,—my father knowing no more about it than I did; notwithstanding he accepted me—sent me to a sword-smith's where I got a sword and sash; he next sent me to a tailor where I got two suits of regimentals; then to the hatters where I got a cap, and a dashing feather which alone cost him ten and sixpence. Equipped for duty, I beat up a few times, but got no recruits, nor in fact did I want any. I was then sent to Stockport, my pay was a guinea per week, and all expences paid on beating up days, which was twice a week. I employed a band of music whenever I beat up, I got a few men here, but they all paid smart, which I always pocketed; this more than doubled my pay.

I had a very narrow escape from drowning in the river which runs by this place; four men and myself went with a large net at midnight to get a draw of fish, when ready for going in, they assured me it was not deep; I had hold of one of the bands, and stepping in was immersed over head, the other four left hold of the net—I could swim, and was determined not to lose the net, but in striving to save myself and it, I got my legs entangled, I struggled with my fate for some time, endeavouring to gain the side, when the current washed the pod of the net so near, that one of the men got hold of it and dragged both me and the net ashore.

From Stockport I was removed to Blackburn, in Lancashire, I was quartered at the three legs of man in Darwin Street; during my stay at this place I attended several oratorios of sacred music, I was acquainted with the chorusses in Handel's Messiah, Haydn's Creation, Judas Maccabeus, Samson, Joshua, Asia and Galatea, &c. At my quarters I considered myself a gentleman, and paid for my board accordingly,—but I ran short of cash here, and receiving an order to repair to the rendezvous in Deansgate, Manchester, I left my sword as a deposit for my bill. When I got to Manchester I told my officer, he blamed me for leaving my sword, saying a publican could not stop a soldier's accoutrements, nor recover a debt amounting to more than one day's pay,—He furnished me with cash, and my sword came by return of coach; my stay at Manchester was short, for Lieut. D. complained of the great expence I had put him to, and had never got him a man, he said he had forty men to raise for a Captaincy, and at my rate of going on they would cost him all his fortune, I demanded the balance of my account, and repairing to rendezvous, broke my sword in two, throwing the pieces on the floor, and desired the Serjeants present to make my respects to Lieutenant D. and tell him my name was *Walker*. From Manchester I took coach to Liverpool being desirous of seeing a sea port, I got among some sailors and among the rest one who advised me to call him my brother in order to deceive his wife, I did so, and we carried on the deception for some time, he used to ask me concerning his uncles, nephews, nieces, &c., but I was under the necessity of *burying them all*, in order to get off with credit, at length my money was again done. I therefore resolved to go on board a man of war.—I had a brother who had been in the navy for many years but I knew not what ship he was in, or where he was stationed. I went to the rendezvous and fearing I might be objected to on account of my fingers, I used the precaution to send for a sheet of writing paper, and scribbling away freely in presence of the master of the gang, I closed, sealed, and directed it to Lord——(the Lord knows who for I do not,) Finsbury square, London. This stratagem had the desired effect—for I no sooner offered my services to the press gang, than every impediment was removed, and I had the pleasure of hearing it whispered "He is a scholar, he will do for captain's clerk, or purser's steward."—I was conducted to the regulating captain, who seeing me in serjeant's uniform suspected I had come to obtain leave to go on board the guard ship, to search for deserters; but on my informing him I was a gentleman's son in disguise, the press master whispered to the captain, "Please your honor, he wrote a letter to a *Lord* this morning." The captain assured me I should certainly rise to "Fame, honor, and preferment." I was sent on board the

Princess—no sooner did the ship's crew and volunteers see me on board than they concluded as the captain had done, and I saw several sneak away down below; presently upon hearing the truth of the matter, an old seaman came behind me and cut off my jacket laps, I was then conducted down into the press room where there was a sort of mock trial to undergo. Several old sailors had placed themselves to the right and left of an old weather-beaten tar—this son of Neptune was elevated above the rest, he had I think at least half an ounce of tobacco in his mouth, after rolling his quid, he addressed the jurymen as follows, " brother shipmates, you see as how this land crab has crawled on board this here ship, and has done nothing but crawl along shore before, therefore before he be free of the sea and has liberty to box his *arse* against salt water, it is necessary he should pay the usual fee, which is one shilling, to drink the health of His Majesty King George the third." The jurymen laid their heads together and presently brought in their verdict accordingly. I paid the shilling, took a chew of tobacco out of the President's box, and the ceremony was over. On going on deck, the Purser's steward gave me a bed and blanket, charging me to watch it closely, or that some of the old hands would steal it; in order to prevent this I sat upon it;—not long after a lighter with water came alongside, and all hands were called to clear her, this being done I returned to where I had left my bed, but the *bird had flown*. I thought I would try to get another when the beds were piped down, and no sooner did the Boatswain's mate's pipe go, but I took the first that came in my way. An old seaman who was in the Princess was draughted with me (as will afterwards appear) on board the Glory, 98 guns, and he there shewed me my blanket and ten others which he had stolen; he had taken the flocks out of the bed and stuffed the tick with blankets in lieu. At night we were all locked down in the press room;—the old hands were allowed hammocks, but the Johnny raws were obliged to plank it on the deck. During the night a large tub which stood for convenience in the middle of the room was upset, being nearly full, it set our beds, clothes, &c., on float. The men in the hammocks had fish hooks fastened to lines which they threw out and hooked our blankets, and so drew them up into their hammocks; their appeared to be no redress, as we were in the dark. A poor black fellow had made a complaint the day before against a seaman, three or four of the latter had provided themselves with pieces of rope, and knowing where he lay, got out of their hammocks and beat him about the press room naked, until the poor fellow bawled out, " murder, tree pon won, dey murder me." The Lieutenant came down with a lantern and a drawn sword, but all were (apparently) sound asleep.—Two men attempted to make their escape in the evening by swimming, but were detected and put in *limbo* until they were sent round with myself and many more, (in the whole ninety some were impressed and others volunteers;—we were sent on board the Rosa Tender, Lieut. Mercer, Commander, and ordered to Plymouth.—We passed the Black Rocks, and saw a great number of porpoises sporting in the water. When we were in sight of Holyhead we saw a vessel which our officers deemed a smuggler, and made sail after her, but she was too light in her heels; we put into Holyhead and anchored, Lieutenat M. and his wife went on shore. The men in the press room had secretly agreed to take the boats at seven that evening, and a signal was appointed, when the bell struck, some hands being on deck were to sing out rusty lock, upon which the rest were to jump on deck, and securing such of the tender's crew as were opposed to it, make their way to the shore, and dividing themselves into parties, proceed over the mountains in Wales; at seven about ten men sang out rusty lock, but not a man offering to come on deck, they were glad to get below again,—the ship's company took no notice. Next morning the smuggler we had chased was recognized on the sands, a boat was sent to overhaul her, but to no purpose, she had taken advantage of the *darkey*, and had discharged her cargo; they made a present of a small keg to the boat's crew, but as the men gave the officer a *so so* character, the master of the smuggler would give him nothing, we sailed for Plymouth, and arrived after a pleasant cruise. We were put on board the Salvador del Mundo, guard ship in Hamoaze, a standing order on board which ship was, that the men were to be clean shaved twice a week; a poor barber had been impressed and not having a razor he substituted a knife; I lathered and he shaved no less than thirty-five one afternoon, each man paying half a pint of wine for a scrape. A few days after twenty of us were picked out to go on board the Glory, 98; she was cruising in the channel; we set sail and joined her—no sooner had we got on board than we were ranked on the quarter deck to get hammocks and bags. The doctor inspected us, I thought he fixed his eyes on me, and a person in uniform came up to me saying, " is your name William Brown." I replied, " yes, and by G— you are my brother." (I mentioned him before) I thought it very singular to meet one that I had not seen for so many years, he was Captain's clerk an excellent penman and a Watchmaker by trade, he conducted me to his cabin and fetched out the rum bottle, the first thing he said to me when somewhat composed, was, " William I had rather have seen you hung than see you in a man of war," I replied " Harry, it's all the fortune of war," my meeting him was of service to me as he got me to assist him in the office. After cruising in the channel a few weeks we were ordered home to Portsmouth where we refitted with all expedition for foreign service. Sir John Orde, Vice Admiral, hoisted his flag on board of us, and in a few days we sailed for Cadiz—this was on the first of November, 1804.

In the Bay of Biscay, we fell in with and brought to a ship under Spanish colours; we had no instructions to take Spanish vessels, though we expected to go to war with that nation every day; she professed to be loaded with Hides and Tallow. Captain Craven turned the hands up to know whether, in the event of detaining her, they would agree to pay *their shares*, if he was adjudged to pay damages for unlawfully detaining her; they to a man agreed—however his timidity overcame him, and he let her go. A few days after we had the mortification to hear the sea horse frigate, had fallen in with her the day after and carried her into port, where she was adjudged a lawful prize, and no less than forty chests of dollars were found concealed under the hides and tallow.

We continued our voyage, a gale of wind came on and a thick haze, so that we could scarcely see one another; this continued two or three days, the sea raged with incredible fury, and we had reason to believe we were near the land. The first Lieutenant P——d, placed a bottle of rum and half-a-guinea under it on the binnacle, which the Quarter Master lashed there for the man who should first discover land. It was impossible to keep the men from the mast heads, dangerous as their situation was; at length the fog suddenly gave way, and a man at the foretopmast head hailed the man at the main, saying, "Tom, don't you think that's land," "where," said Tom. "Right a-head," said the former. Tom looked—caught hold of the back stay, jumped on deck, and seized the bottle.— "What are you going to do with that," said the Quarter Master, " Oh by G—," he replied " I had forgot, down with the helm or we shall all be on shore"; on looking, the bluff land of Cape Spartel, was right a-head, and we were within a few minutes sail, scudding right before it; the helm was righted, and we entered the gut of Gibraltar; the gale had rather increased than abated. We kept Apes' Hill and Ceuta Point as near as possible, when opposite the Bay of Gibralter we set a new main storm stay-sail, but had no sooner belayed the sheet, than it blew into baby rags. Capt. Craven, at this critical moment, said "turn the hands up that they may see their danger," at which the bulk of the ship's company ridiculed him, calling him an old washerwoman, &c. if there were no worse Captains than Craven was in the Navy, in war time volunteers would be more plentiful, and the national stain of impressing men would be completely done away. Allow me to name a single instance or two of the humanity of Capt. C.—A bad man was reported for drunkenness, he was brought to the gangway and seized up; the Captain asked the man if any of the ship's company would say anything in his favor—all were silent,—"Will any of your messmates?"—all silent, "What" said the Captain, "will no man stand your friend?" "No sir," said the man, "Then I'll stand your friend," said the Captain, "cast him loose." Another instance is, a man was reported for being below in his watch, and when about to be punished, informed the Captain he had been very unwell during his confinement. "Why did you not go to the doctor," said Captain C. "I thought you would think I had done it to escape punishment, sir." "I like that principle," said the Captain, "go down below."

Just as the sail blew away the Spaniards fired at us

from Ceuta Point,—" look at the cowardly rascals," (said the Captain) "firing at a ship in distress,"—we however succeeded in getting into Tetuan Bay and moored.

A few days after we received instructions to take, sink, burn, and destroy all vessels belonging to his most Excellent Catholic Majesty. A short time after we took our station off Cadiz—we were five line of battle ships and a frigate; we kept cruising off until the ninth of April, 1805, when a number of victuallers arrived from Gibraltar, the squadron stood in shore and anchored near the light house; each ship had a victualler alongside, and another astern; we got our empty water and provision casks on the booms, and had our main deck covered with full water casks,—provisions, &c. A minute gun was heard in the direction of the gut. I was signal man to Sir John at this time, and was at the mast head, so was Mr. Dowers flag Lieutenant, the firing continuing and approaching nearer by the sound, a large ship was seen standing towards us under a press of sail, she proved to be the Renown, 74, with the signal flying for an enemy in sight, Sir John, inquired by Telegraph, "are the enemy superior to us in point of number?" the answer from the Renown was, " yes," Sir John, inquired again, " can we engage the enemy with any probable hope of success?"—the answer was " No." Shortly we observed eleven sail of the line, several frigates, two brigs, and a corvette. My shipmates informed me at this moment Sir John sheathed his sword, saying he would never draw it in defence of his country again. I was told his reason was, he had received private intelligence of this fleet coming from Toulon, and had requested a reinforcement which the Lords of the Admiralty would not, or at least had not complied with, in addition to this fleet there were thirteen sail of the line, French and Spanish, laying in Cadiz Bay, ready for sea, and were actually under weigh every day, they would stand out to the harbour's mouth and then stand in again. I beg leave to observe, since my residence at this place, being within two or three miles of Sir John's late residence (Bolton Hall), I have been chagrined to hear many charging Sir John with cowardice on this occasion.—I will now, for the justification of the Vice Admiral and Commander in Chief of the British squadron alluded to, name (from memory) two of his standing orders, the first was to engage the enemy whenever it could be done with the least probable hope of success, the second was to avoid as much as possible the effusion of human blood, here I think is unity of courage, humanity, and prudence, and his language is a standard worthy any British Officer. I have known a fool hardy, madcap C. E. F. I have known a Sir S. S. and others who to gain a very insignificant advantage, would run the risk of losing both ships and men, but more of this hereafter. The Admiral ordered the water casks to be thrown overboard, we stove in the heads of them, letting the water out at the scuppers, and overboard they went, the Spaniards in their boats were on the alert and toggling six or eight together towed them ashore,

The squadron was cleared for action, we made the signal to get under weigh, the anchors being catted, we stood for England. A French frigate stood in for Cadiz Bay, the next day we fell in with a merchant vessel, a cabin boy got into the mizen chains and hailed her—" board a ship a-hoy, hollo, what, have you heard the news ?" " No, sir," " why we've made the French fleet run," " I'm glad to hear it sir," " ah but," said the boy " 'twas after us." The boy was overheard, called inboard and got a severe flogging. We joined the channel fleet and gave the intelligence, Capt. Craven, at his request was superannuated and made Governor of Haslar Hospital, my brother also (his Clerk) got his discharge per request. Sir John Orde after turning the hands up and thanking them for their good behaviour, promised to secure to the men what prize money he could, (The Defence, Ruby, Polyphemus, and Swiftsure had taken several galleons and the squadron had agreed to share, but I believe none of the Glory's men ever got as much as would pay turnpike for a walking stick. I am sure I never did,) and left the ship and I believe never joined one afterwards, but on his landing finding there were many aspersions, bitter sarcasms, and ungenerous reflections afloat, demanded a court of enquiry on his conduct, when the result was he was honorably acquitted. Rear-Admiral T. next hoisted his flag on board of us and we were sent in quest of a flying squadron commanded by a brother of N. Bonaparte's. One evening our look out men descried a vessel, coming down before the wind, we were close hauled, we got our bow guns ready and fired at her as she crossed our bow, a frigate was closely pursuing her, we hailed the frigate, ordering the Captain to heave to—he hailed us in return and said he had been in chase of the brig that had passed us eighteen hours and was fast coming up with her, "heave too and come on board" replied our Captain, he did so, and was ordered to keep company during the night, in the morning he had the pleasure of seeing his prize taken in tow by the Barfleur, 98,—our Admiral ordered him to take possession of the prize, he then with his prize parted company. A few days after about 6 p. m. a frigate under English colours was seen to be chased by another frigate, we all stood towards them, the Mars 74, being the best sailing ship got considerably a-head of the squadron, she made the signal for an enemy's squadron of four frigates, we were guided by her motions, but night coming on we mistook her signal, which was to continue in the same position, and mistaking it for the signal to alter our course, we tacked and next morning had nothing in sight but our own ships,—the Mars was wanting, being recalled and ordered to Plymouth, two days after we had the pleasure of seeing the Mars arrive with a frigate in tow, some of the crew of the Mars gave me the following account. " After losing sight of our squadron we continued the chase until break of day, the four french frigates upon seeing only a single ship, formed the order of battle in two lines, the captain of the Mars in order to deceive the enemy, hoisted a signal and fired a gun, they concluded our squadron was in sight; on the Mars running in between them to break their line, she fired a broadside into each of the sternmost ships, the two headmost made all sail as did the weathermost of the other two, the fourth after another broadside struck and we took possession of her." We were ordered round to Long-Reach where we got our guns out and were draughted into different ships, and the Glory was laid up being unfit for further service, I was sent in company with the band and a few favorites to St. Helens as supernumeraries, to join the Lively for a passage to Lisbon to wait the arrival of the Barfleur, which ship we were appointed to. After going to the dock yard at Portsmouth and receiving our wages we returned on board, and Rear-Admiral W. A. Otway hoisted his first flag (blue at the mizen), we weighed anchor and stood down channel with a snug topgallant breeze. We had a rough passage, at length we made Cape Finisterre, but it was with the greatest difficulty we weathered it. A ship by night ran athwart our bows, right before the wind, the crew seemed to have lost all command of her and although we fired guns, blew the bugles, and beat the drum, she continued her course and must inevitably have been dashed to pieces, being within ten minutes sail of the Cape right a-head. The day following the man at the mast head reported a strange fleet—this proved to be the Burling Rocks, projecting considerably out of the water. We joined the squadron off Lisbon, and the supernumeraries were put on board the Ganges, 74, Capt. Peter Halket, not (as some have called him) Hell Cat. We had a very unpleasant time on board this ship, Capt. H. being an old Post Captain and W. A. O. but had just received his first flag, he punished two or three of our men the Admiral not liking to interfere, in a short time the Barfleur came out and we joined her, our *Captain was S. H. L. I hope he is at rest, but he would suffer no man to be so while living. The Russian fleet, had passed and was overhauled by us while cruising off Cadiz, they were anchored in the Tagus. The French were attempting to get possession of Lisbon, but upon Sir C. C. and Dal——e converting their swords into *Pens* the French were allowed to depart with the honors of war. We entered the Tagus and supplying the Russian ships (seven in number) with one month's provisions each we took charge of them, they had two unfit for sea which were dismantled and laid up in Jack-ass Bay. Our squadron and the Russians put to sea together the Russian Admiral keeping the weathergage, nothing particular transpired on the passage save firing a few shot to make the Russians' keep there stations, when our arrival was announced at the Isle of Wight, the Admiral from the Royal William, sent his Tender out with an order for the Rear Admiral to demand all the Russians' ammunition, &c., upon receiving this order we expected resistance on the part of the Russians and our squadron cleared for action, however they gave up all quietly. They had orders also not to hoist their

* This Captain did not join us at this time, it was D. M. C. L'd a worthy man.

colours, and the English commander out of courtesy to the Russian Admiral did not hoist his, it was a rare sight to see fourteen line of battle ships coming into an English harbour without a single flag flying, the Russian ships moored at the Mother Bank, and were to remain there until six months after peace between the two powers, at the expiration of which time they were to be given up in as good condition as we found them, a Russian frigate and a store ship, arrived and anchored at Spithead, the captain of the frigate went ashore, the frigate contained money to a great amount, the signal was made to watch her motions, and the captain returning early in the morning slipt one of his cables, on which the Topaz frigate's signal was made to weigh and drop alongside the Russian frigate. The signal was next to send boats manned and armed on board of her, all was in motion and boats were going in every direction, boarding in twenty different parts of the ship at the same moment.—The ship's crew of the frigate, finding they were taken, cut the throats of what sheep and pigs were on board and eat them raw. There were sixty seven pendant ships that shared for the two prizes. We were dispatched to resume our station off Lisbon, we cruised awhile in company with the Resolution, Ruby, Ganges, and others, it was about this time Captain S. H. L. joined us, he had been but a short time with us before he alarmed the ship's company by his expressions; we were sent to Ferrol to fit out the Spanish ships laying there, as the French were in Spain, and the latter were in alliance with us at that

E

time, this service being performed we afterwards went to Vigo Bay, with a large fleet of transports, from whence we sailed to Corunna, it was in the vicinity of this place that Sir John Moore was killed in action, and (if I recollect right) Sir David Baird lost an arm, the firing was distinctly heard by the ship's crews in the Bay, it ceased towards evening, and the whole of the night was occupied by boats taking in and bringing our troops on board, who had retreated into the town during the night, it would be presumptuous in me to attempt to give any correct idea of the horrid state the army was in. If hunger, nakedness, fatigue, and wounds argue misery they possessed a large share, we repaired with them to Plymouth. At the time we left the Bay of Corunna, the French were bombarding the town—we had taken a poor woman on board, she had a child not bigger than my fist, it was only three days old when brought on board. The mother gave us the following relation, " being with my husband, I grew fatigued and could follow the army no further, I laid down and was immediately delivered, no person being at hand, by and bye the advanced guard of the enemy came up, some baggage waggons followed, there were some French women with the waggons. A French soldier came up to me, took my infant by one leg, drew is sword and was just going to cleave it in two, when a woman arrested his arm. General Junot, upon hearing I was in the camp, sent for me and gave me a note addressed to Sir John Moore, stating his having arrived with a reinforcement of 15,000 men, before I could get to join the

English Army, the action commenced and my husband was nearly the first man that fell." She had much kindness shewn her on board by the only woman we had in the ship, but when we arrived at Plymouth, and landed her on shore, it was proved to a demonstration that the loss of her husband had not had much effect upon her, she had secreted about her person, property worth upwards of two hundred pounds, which she had got by prowling over and robbing the dead and dying in the field of battle. The soldiers had the middle deck to themselves, and such was their exhausted state, that on coming on board they threw themselves down upon the deck, and when endeavours were made to arouse them, we could not do it, several were picked out from among them dead, and thrown overboard. I was assisting the Purser's steward to form them into messes, and observing a man bent nearly double, I asked him what was the matter, he answered by nothing but deep groans. I desired his comrades to convey him to the sick-bay, which they did. The Docter asked him what was the matter, the groans continued, " take him away said the *humane doctor*, let him lay down, he is fatigued that's all," upon which he fixed his eyes upon the doctor, and three times (evidently in the agonies of death) exclaimed " d—n you, d—n you, d—n you,"—he fell a lifeless corpse, the surgeon's assistant said, " the man's dead sir," " well" replied the doctor, " why don't you tie his toes together."—Some time after the Barfleur, came into Cawsand Bay, and the ship's company, not approving of their captain, wrote a letter secretly to the

Admiralty requesting a new captain, I believe no attention was paid to the first, they wrote again, whether a third letter was written or not I will not presume to say, as I never was consulted nor had I ever the least knowledge by whom they were wrote or sent, the last letter was to the following effect. " We are willing to go wherever his Majesty's service requires, if your Lordships will be pleased to appoint any other captain, but before we will sail with him we will sink at our anchors." The port Admiral and three post captains came on board, turned the hands up and asked the men separately, if they knew any thing of the letters in question, all were silent, " has any man any thing to say against Captain L.?" no answer, the men went down below, the Admiral and Captains, went into the captain's cabin, and when coming out again on the quarter deck, the whole ship's company (nearly to a man) ran upon deck, and with general consent cried out, " a new captain."—The captain came out foaming like a bull, drew his sword and charged the men with wounding him in the nicest part, saying they had attacked him unfairly, &c., the Sunday following he went on shore, leaving orders with Lieutenant Le Mesurier to muster the ship's company, and see if he could discover the writers of the letters, the Lieutenant did as directed, the ship's company was mustered on the quarter deck, the letters read, and the question asked, "does any of you know any thing of the letters now read?" no answer, Captain L. had commanded the Mars, 74, previous to his joining the Barfleur, and we had a draft of her men on board, this led to a suspicion that they had wrote the letters, while this process was going on a midshipman observed to the 1st. Lieutenant, "there's Bennett sir, has sailed with Captain L. and wishes to speak," "come forward Bennett," said the Lieutenant, "have you any thing to say against Capt. L.?" he taking his hat off, said (with a low bow) " I have only to say sir, I have sailed with Captain L. before and never wish to sail with him again," here it rested for the present. On the captain's coming on board in the evening the 1st. Lieutenant reported what had transpired; the captain turned the hands up and placing Bennett and Jones on the quarter deck, on the weather side, assured them he would hang them if possible, after an harangue the men were sent below except Bennett and Jones, who were ordered in Irons for mutiny, the charge against the latter was for crying out a new captain, on the day the port Admiral was on board, an order for a court martial was immediately obtained as the ship was wanted for service. The court martial was ordered, and the Judge Advocate came on board to converse with and give the prisoners notice for trial. The day previous to the court martial, towards evening, the first Lieutenant sent the Pinnace with witnesses, marines, prisoners, and boat's crew, from Cawsand Bay to Hamoaze, in all two and twenty souls.—It was not until the gun sounded the next morning from the Salvador del Mundo, that I was sent with the clerk, taking the ship's books with us, to prove that the prisoners belonged to the ship, when to our sorrow we learnt that the Pinnace had upset rounding

Penley Point, and seventeen out of the twenty-two were drowned. Jones was one of them; Bennett had struggled with his fate near two hours, (the boat was keel up,) and though a good swimmer, he was near drowning from others seizing him by the legs, arms, &c., and he was under the necessity of cutting them with his knife in order to disentangle himself from them.—When he got hold of the keel, a spray would wash him off again. He was a messmate of mine, and I had made his defence for him, which he had in his waistcoat pocket during the time he was in the water; at length a boat from Plymouth sound went at the hazard of the Men's lives and saved the surviving five. Many friends of the deceased had come many miles to see their husbands, brothers, children, &c.; the bodies were constantly floating ashore at high water. The court martial being assembled, the prisoner Bennett was called into court, he appeared pale as ashes; on the president's observing which, he told him he did not appear in a fit state to take his trial, the court would therefore grant him a few days to recruit his strength. Bennett thanked him, telling him he wished the court martial to proceed, as he would give the court no additional trouble. The court proceeded and when called upon for his defence the Judge Advocate read it, every officer in the ship gave him a good character, with the exception of the captain, who attempted to speak, but was called to silence by the president, who said he had brought the man to try him for his life, his character of him therefore was unnecessary. The man was immediatly discharged, but Captain L. took him ashore at Cadiz, and he deserted shortly after.

The day after, the signal was made to weigh anchor when the whole of the ship's company went down below and lowered the lower deck ports; the signal was made for mutiny and marines came from the Invincible, Mars, Zealous, Ville de Paris, &c., the master came down below and attempted to address the ship's company, but was hissed at; the first Lieutenant (a man much respected) came down and with tears in his eyes, said, " my men, will you hear me?"—silence was ordered, when he informed the ship's company that Captain L. was superseded in the command of the Barfleur, and Sir Thomas Masterman Hardy, from the Triumph, was to command her; this news was received with three cheers—and up anchor was the word; it was up in a trice, and we set sail for Lisbon. On our passage out, (I was then a writer in the office,) Captain L. came into the office one morning, and asked me what I was about; I told him cleaning the office;—he said he believed me to be a " d—n mutinous scoundrel," now thought I, if I don't fly into a great passion he will certainly conclude me guilty, when striking the desk with my fist as hard as I could, " no, sir" said I, " I never was a mutinous scoundrel in my life, if you consider me such, try me by a court martial, or if any one has said any thing to you injurious to my character (which I suspect they have) take me in private and I'll give you an explanation." He replied, he wanted none of my explanations, and walked away. He called his servant into the after cabin one day, and asked him if he had cleaned his boots. "Yes, sir," "do they shine?" "velly well, sir." "Did you brush my coat Pierre Filtz?" "yes, sir." "Tell Mr. Le Mesurier I shall be glad of his company to breakfast" "yes, sir." The servant returned:—"well, will he come?" "yes, sir," much obliged to you sir," "Filtz, I like you very well," "tank you, sir." "You are a good servant,"—"tank you sir." At this moment the captain sprung up, took down his sword, and ran after Poor Filtz, spitting at him and swearing he would cut his bloody black head off; the poor fellow in his fright knocked my table over in the fore cabin, and bursting the door open ran on the quarter deck. The captain called to the sentinel to know the reason he did not open the door to his servant, then going into his cabin, set up a loud laugh, saying he had frightened the black rascal terribly.

At length we arrived at Lisbon, and the next day Sir Thomas came on board and read his commission, he brought about 80 men with him, and Captain L. took as many with him into the Triumph, not because it was their wish, but his; I was among the number of his followers, but would rather have been a thousand miles another way, though I did not say a single word.

We were dispatched in consequence of having heard there were two French line of battle ships at sea which had made their escape from Toulon. We went to Madeira, and the captain, as was his custom, called me into his cabin, bidding me bring paper, pen, &c., I did,

He was in his cot and I had to kneel and write the following as he dictated it.

Sir,

Should your excellency be in possession of any intelligence, respecting the two French line of battle ships, Polonois and Courageux, supposed to be bound to a port in France, and of whom I am in search, you will please to communicate the same to me for the benefit of His Majesty's service.

I am,
Your Excellency's
Most obedient servant,
S. H. L.

To His Excellency the Commander
in Chief at Madeira, or to the
Senior Officer of H.M. Ships and
vessels which are, or may hereafter arrive at that anchorage.

The Dottrell sloop of war, was in company and dispatched with this letter while we were cruising off.—The commander made all sail, and lay to off Madeira Roads. He sent the letter on shore instantly. We hoisted the recall and fired minute guns, then filled and stood to the eastward, the recall still flying and the minute guns continuing;—the sloop made all possible sail, but could not keep up owing to our superiority in sailing and it blowing a stiff breeze. At length we hove to and made signal for the captain. As soon as he came on board he was ordered aft, and kept there two hours, some of the sloop's crew, had contrived to forward a letter to Captain L., complaining of ill treatment, &c., when we arrived at Lisbon, (having received intelligence that the French ships, had got into port,) Captain L. tried him by a court martial, and he was dismissed the service.—He came home in plain clothes, a passenger in our ship.

It is certainly worthy of remark, that Captain L. who a few months before had been dismissed his ship, should be the first to try another on the same charge and get him dismissed—some time after this we were sent to join the fleet in Cadiz Bay; we had scarcely arrived when we were ordered to destroy Fort Catalina, it stood opposite the town, and mounted heavy brass pieces. I went with the men's grog one day, and just as I had served it out, the French were seen coming in vast numbers towards us, their bayonets and swords glittering in the sun, we made to our boats as quick as possible, but had scarcely got out of gun shot, when the enemy were on the ruins of the Fort, and had their field pieces upon the beach. We had succeeded in destroying the embrasures, and had thrown the guns into the sea, but the French contrived to get them up again, and to repair all damages; they took possession of St. Mary's and Fort Louis. We had a small battery on the Peninsula, leading to Fort Louis;—opposite to this was the Spanish Fort Matagorda. The French made several attempts to get to Cadiz, but the activity of the Spaniards in building sand batteries, &c., across the pass leading to the Citadel did them infinite credit.

was on shore, and saw high and low, Friars and Laymen, for a distance of at least a quarter of a mile, handing the sand bags from one to another. Our flat bottomed boats, up the creek, annoyed the enemy much in their endeavours to build a battery within reach of the one we occupied. We had also a Spanish block ship, the St. Just, near our battery moored with springs on her cables and manned by the ships of the fleet.

A midshipman of ours with five others (up the creek) went on shore near the enemy, having no arms with them; after walking about some time and seeing nothing, one of the men said, " should a guard of French men come we should be in a nice hobble, we had better get some sticks, or any thing we can find;" they picked up an old bayonet and any thing that they could get. At this moment one of the men saw a French soldier come out of a house close by them; the midshipman said, if they offered to run they were sure to be shot by the guard (for they now perceived it was a guard house), " let us go," said he, " and take them by surprise." They instantly rushed to the door and commanded them to surrender, which they immediately did (not knowing their force), and having tied them together, brought them out, when they saw our force they cursed like what they were. Our men handed them into the boat and brought them aboard, there were twelve men, and a serjeant and corporal, for this rash step the midshipman was severely reprimanded, though we could not but applaud his courage and presence of mind.

One morning at day break we were alarmed by a dreadfull report of an explosion; we discovered the guard house, which had been so much annoyed by the block ship and battery, completely razed to the ground, but the enemy had completed their design, for inside they had a complete battery for heating red hot shot, they commenced their fire upon the block ship, cut her cables, and set her on fire in several places; she drifted and it was with much difficulty we could get our men out of her. They then began with our eight gun battery, which was nobly defended, even when battered to shatters, by an Irish Captain, who swore he never would strike while we would supply him with ammunition. We got the men away and the French took possession. The French had taken Cadiz a short time before, but the Spaniards rose armed *en masse* and put the former to the route. Our squadron was then cruising in the offing, and a flag of truce was sent out by the Spaniards, inviting us to enter the Bay, but it was not until the batteries opened fire upon the French shipping that we could believe the Spaniards sincere. Our shipping then entered. The dreadful usage of the Spaniards to the prisoners on board the ships was perhaps without parallel. I am aware how severely the former had been injured by the latter; yet to picture to one's self a company of from twelve to sixteen hundred men crammed together in a ship, nearly without any support, sickness and disease raging in all their horrid forms, and scarcely any thing to cover their nakedness; such was their condition. They were supplied with their scanty pittance from the shore. I have seen an empty water cask suspended by a rope to a jury-mast-head three days successively, this was a signal to denote want of water, there was scarcely a morning that we did not witness some thrown overboard, having died from want or suffocation.

The Spaniards frequently suspended their dead bodies, by swab robes round their necks, dangling in the water, until the bodies were completely putrified; often have obscure individuals swam to our ships, and getting on board, have prostrated themselves with their faces on the ground praying the merciful interference of the English, they were generally refreshed by the ships' companies, but were returned to their ships next morning. The prisoners had contrived to convey a letter to our Admiral praying relief, he remonstrated with the Spanish Government but to little or no purpose.

I remember a letter coming from one of their ships, threatening in the event of obtaining no relief, to cut the cables the first favorable wind, and drift over to the French, though they should be sunk by the English ships in the attempt; a day or two after, a boat with provisions came alongside, and the Frenchmen jumped down the ship's side to hand it up, there were two soldiers in the boat with bayonets fixed, to protect the boat and a steersman, about twenty prisoners jumped into the boat, cast her off, and ordered the steersman to steer for St. Mary's, they filled their sail and the wind being fair they were out of the reach of our guns before we could fire at them, boats were sent after them in every direction, and the steersman observing this put the helm down and was for beating back again, upon which one of the prisoners seized one of the sentinel's musquets and running him through the body with his bayonet, threw him overboard, he righted the helm and succeeded in reaching the opposite shore where they were protected by field pieces, and welcomed on shore by their countrymen.

I cannot suffer to pass unnoticed here, the treachery and duplicity of a Lieutenant commanding one of our flat bottomed boats up the creek, he could speak French, and observing a sentinel walking on his post on the French lines, he hoisted a white handkerchief, hailed the sentinel and pretended they had deserted the English and wanted protection, the man laid down his musquet and was advancing towards the boat, we had a sixpounder in the bow of the boat, by the officer's direction it was fired and the man blown to atoms, the enemy behind a thicket were on the look out—they brought a field piece to the beach, fired, and took a leg each off two of our men; how different the following, a Lieutenant in the same service, observing some French officers on shore, took out his handerchief and waved it as a token of friendship, the French did the same, he then took a bottle of wine and drank their healths, they also took out a bottle and returned the compliment, they again mutually waved their handkerchiefs and retired.

A heavy gale of wind coming on and blowing over

to St. Mary's, a number of vessels drifted from their anchors, thirty merchant vessels drifted over to the French, as did also the San Roman, a Spanish 74, the latter was set on fire by the enemy, and burnt to the water's edge. The crew of the San Roman had deserted her. We were informed there was in her hold a great quantity of quicksilver, silver plate, &c. At midnight we sent a boat with a spar, blocks, &c., and a party of men who could dive well; they succeeded in getting a quantity of silver plate, dishes, urns, &c., and a large quantity of quicksilver in boxes, enclosed in three leathers each, and sealed at the top—there were 50lbs in each skin. This was repeated, unknown to any of the other ships, for several evenings; the men considering second plunder as good as the first, embezzled all they could, and sold it to the purser for liquor. I purchased one evening three hundred ounces of silver, at three shillings per ounce, for the said purser—it consisted of three dozen plates. Our men had made too free with the quicksilver, some put it in their mouths, some cleaned their tin lamps with it, and no sooner did they light them than the quicksilver melted the solder and the lamps fell from their sockets. The marine guard thinking they had found a readier way of polishing their buttons, touched them over with it, but when mounting guard on the quarter deck, they found no remains of their buttons but the shanks, in fact, most of the ship's company were in a state of salivation. There was an officer every night to see the quicksilver handed up the ship's side, and to see it put under safe custody. One night I was walking with S. C. B. captain's clerk, on the quarter deck, and Mr. B. master of the ship was officer on watch, the boat arrived, hands were ordered to hand up the skins and lay them on the quarter deck ; Mr. B. stood over them, swearing, if any one did him they had but another to do,—and that was the d——l. I said to the clerk, " I'll have one of the skins ;" when putting my hand between his legs (as he stood with his back to me) I took one, put it under my jacket, and going down below, *planted* it. I soon came up again and asked Mr. B. if all was right, he said, " yes." Shortly after he said to me rather boldly, " Brown take one of these skins down below for me," " by whose orders?" said I, " Mr. B's," said he; upon which I took another as I thought unperceived, and carried it to the clerk's servant down in the cockpit. While there I heard the quarter-master calling for me, he said the master had been informed by a midshipman that I had carried a skin of quicksilver down below. I asked, " what are they doing with it now ?" "they are carrying it below into the gun room," said he, " that will do," said I. Then taking the skin from the servant, I ran upon the main deck to the sentinel at the cabin door, giving him the quicksilver, charging him to mind I had given it him. I then proceeded to the quarter deck, when going up to the master, I said, " Pray did you send for me, sir?" " me send for you, sir yes, pray did you take a skin of quicksilver from off the quarter deck?" " yes, sir," " How durst you do it?" "why, sir, I had little to do, and thought I might as well carry one down as not, sir." "Pray, what did you do with it?" "took it to the sentinal at the gun room door sir," "you did?" "yes, sir." Where is the midshipman of the watch?" "Here, sir." "Go to the sentinel, and ask him if Brown brought a skin of quicksilver to him or not?" the midshipman returned. "Well what does he say?" "He says, yes sir, he took it from himself." "Sir," said I, "I am sorry you should for a moment suspect my honesty." "Why," said he, "I could not believe it, but there are such a set of scoundrels about me, that they would steal a man's eye tooth. I am sorry I should think hardly of you; go down to my steward and tell him to give you some grog." All this time I had my skin safe enough. However the effects of the quicksilver became alarming among the men, and our captain wrote to the Admiral, saying, he had picked up a quantity of quicksilver from the wreck of the San Roman, and wished to know how he was to dispose of it. The Admiral issued a circular, demanding what quantity each ship had picked up. I believe no ship had any of it but ours. News was communicated to the Spanish authorities, who sent hands on board, re-packed it and took it on shore. I believe our return to the Admiral, was not half of what was on board, the remainder was secreted.

Our ship was ordered round to Gibraltar to clear out, every kind of provision being tainted with quicksilver. There was a merchant vessel lying close to us in Cadiz Bay, upon hearing of our removal to Gibraltar, she got under weigh and was there nearly as soon as we were; the master of this vessel had traded largely with our officers in the above line, and had perhaps been invited to follow. Upon arriving at the Bay of Gibraltar I was employed every night, for several nights, filling lime juice bottles and handing them out of the gun-room ports, into a boat belonging to the above vessel.

Three hundred of our men were put on board two transports and ninety were sent to the hospital; we were lashed to the jetty ashore; we cleared her out entirely; the shingle ballast was washed, &c. The master caulker Mr. S. had got scent that the men of our ship had quicksilver to dispose of, and he whispered among the men that he would give them ten dollars per skin for it. He bought a great quantity. I had so much to do with it that it threw me ill. The day prior to this I had given two skins to a shipmate to carry to Mr. S.; his sheds were close to the jetty, and his (Mr. S's) custom was to receive the stuff one day taking the names, and pay the day following.

The next morning in company with many more I was sent to the hospital,—as we were going up Scud Hill, I slipt into a grog shop, the doctor observed me, and seizing me by the neck marched me off to the hospital.

Our second Lieutenant Mr. J. and the master fought a duel on the rock, the former was wounded in both thighs and sent to the hospital. Our ward had fourteen beds, and I found lying on each bed a small book; being shewn my bed, I enquired the intention of those books, I was informed the doctor after examining his patients, wrote (for the steward's information,) what diet each man was to have, I got pen and ink and wrote in my book, *full*, upon the doctor coming round and looking at my book, " full,"—said he, " Who wrote this?" " I did, sir," said I, " how dare you do it?" said he, " sir," said I, (very demurely), I thought every man had to put down what he could eat, "I thought I could eat *full*." " Well," said the doctor, "this is a good trick, I thought of putting you upon half, however I will let it stand, and you may have *full*."

I mentioned my having sent two skins of quicksilver to Mr. S.—this I wanted pay for; I sent a note to him requesting payment; he wrote in return, he had not got my name down; I wrote again; he sent, saying he would see me the next morning and give me the satisfaction required. He did not come as proposed, and I sent the following,—" Sir, I expected as a gentleman you would have met me this morning and given me the satisfaction required, I am, &c." I gave this to an old soldier belonging to the veteran battalion to carry (unsealed) to Mr. S.; the soldier set off and had to go through the main guard, when an officer hailed him, asking him where he was going, &c. The soldier, replied, " with a note to the jetty;" when observing it was not sealed, "let me look at it," said he, he took it, and having read the contents, he exclaimed, " another challenge by heaven,"—serjeant put this fellow in the black hole,—he was hurried away, and kept there all night. Next morning a drum-head court martial was called, when the following questions were put to the man;—" who gave you this note?" "A young man in the hospital, Sir." "An officer I suppose?" "I don't know, sir, but I think he is above the common men." "I think so too."—Some officers spoke as to the good character of the soldier;— when the officer said, "take this note back to the hospital, make my compliments to the *gentleman*, and tell him I think there has been duelling enough from H. M. S. Triumph, and if I ever find any challenging again, I will immediately order both parties under an arrest." The poor fellow came to the hospital, and his wife, who was a nurse in our ward, was almost frantic with grief; "what have you done with my poor dear husband?" said she; thus much for the skins of quicksilver.

Having completed our provisions, water, &c. we rejoined the fleet at Cadiz, and from thence went to Lisbon, when I was draughted into the Zealous, 74, Captain Thomas Boys, a worthy man,—the first Lieutenant B——k was not upon the whole a bad fellow, but I thought he often wanted to be down upon me—I never knew his reason. In this ship there were several pious men, they maintained their integrity in spite of every opposition; they had a leader whose name was Samuel Wilton, this man enjoined all who wished to connect themselves with him, to bring their grog upon receiving it, to him, and when all was collected he threw it overboard; this reached the ears of Captain B. who sent for, and required his reasons for so doing; he said, "if a man took a little, that little begat a desire for more, and he thought sin should not be parleyed with." The Captain made him promise to throw no more overboard, saying, " it was part of the men's nourishment and support." After this he collected as usual, and if any had occasion to get their shoes mended or their clothes, they were paid in moderate proportions of grog every morning at four o'clock when going on deck. From my first conversation with this man, he was partial to me, and so were all the members, though my heart was so divided I never joined them; they had their meetings amid the curses and imprecations of the ship's crew,—singing, praying, &c. The Tonnant, Captain Rapier, had a great number of methodists on board, and as she lay alongside of us, we constantly heard them preaching, praying, and singing. On Captain R's. coming on board of us, our Captain asked him how he could carry on duty where there was so much singing; he replied, he wished his ship's company were all the same way disposed, 'for' said he, 'they are the best men in the ship, if overtaken in a gale at sea, I send for the methodists and they are there to a man, when many of the rest are drunk below. It appears to me that there is scarcely ever a good agreement between seamen and marines, though shipmates who have to share the same common danger. Instances might be adduced, let one suffice. A drummer from our ship, his name was Grey—had leave to go on board another ship to see some old shipmates,—he was returned at sunset, (as is customary,) but being very tipsy, the boat's crew pushed him through a port on the lower deck, telling the seamen to take him aft to the marines' birth. This was taken no notice of till we beat to quarters about an hour after, the man being missing was sought for and found under the breast of a gun suffocated; some one informed the captain of the man who was requested to take him up; he sent for him on the quarter deck, asking him his reason for not taking care of the man; the seaman said he thought himself as much above a marine, as the Lord High Admiral was above a journeyman tailor, or the monument above a nine pin.

I spoke in a former part of this work of two Russian ships (unfit for sea) lying in Jack-ass Bay—Marines were sent from each ship in rotation weekly to guard the same. It was our turn to send twelve marines—boys were picked out for the purpose, when the serjeant was warning them to get ready, one whose name was Brown, said, with an oath, he would throw the serjeant overboard before he (Brown) came on board again; they went, and the serjeant with them, Brown was sentry on the gangway, and Coulson at the cabin door; it appeared afterwards, in evidence, that Coulson and Brown had agreed to throw the serjeant overboard—Brown was to make the attempt, and in case of failure, Coulson was to help him. At nine o'clock the serjeant, on going his round with his lantern and candle in his hand, came to Brown, and asked if all was well, Brown replied, "Yes, you old B———r all will be well directly;" so saying, he picked him clean overboard; there being no bulwark to the ship. In he morning, the serjeant (whose name was Holden,) was missing, and all that could be learnt was that he was seen going his rounds at nine o'clock. The marines remained until their week was expired, when they came on board Brown's messmates speaking of the serjeant, said "Brown, you said you would throw him overboard, did you?"—he was speechless; the officers were made acquainted with it, and Brown sent for and examined; upon this Coulson made known the whole affair. They were tried by a court martial, and were hung on board our ship a few days after. A letter was read to the several ships' crews, showing how impossible it was to throw the gates of mercy open to them, having in cool blood and premeditatedly taken the life of a fellow creature without any provocation whatever. Brown's discharge from the service came a few days after he had suffered the penalty of the law.

At this time the French Army was at Villa Franca, and the English at Alhandra, the latter commanded by Wellington, Beresford, and Hill. A number of men were sent as pikemen to co-operate with the army, I was one, and was quartered at a church at Alhandra; when we entered the church there were the Virgin Mary, and a variety of other images, one of my shipmates gave the *Virgin* a slap on the face, and off came her head, (it was made of wax,) "come here, my good fellows" said he, "I have found a good woman;" another took hold of her hand to shake it, and her arm came off. They (or we) took the pipes out of the organ, and marching two and two, blew through them round the town ; (the inhabitants had left)—the French army was within two miles of us. We lay down with our arms, a cutlass, brace of pistols, and a pike—and were roused up every morning at day break for inspection; our employment through the day, was pulling down houses, building mud batteries, &c. We were sometimes building walls across the road between the enemy and us, to impede the progress of their horse, in the event of an attack. Upon the army arriving here the place was stowed with wine, our soldiers began to make too free with it and a party was sent to stove all the vats. We had a number of flat bottomed boats in the Tagus, our men suffered much from the flux occasioned by eating unripe figs, oranges, and drinking new wine. Our food was very indifferent having no regular way of cooking it, and most of our beef and pork was eaten raw. The officers were as bad off as the men, and if we could get hold of a pig or bullock, would very readily join at either.

One day three men belonging to one of the flat boats went to forage, they fell in with a pig and ran after it, one of the men threw himself across its back, his shipmate, Patrick Bryan, being about twenty yards off, presented a pistol, crying out, " hold him fast and I'll shoot him," he fired, and fortunately shot the pig through the neck, and ran up to it, when a captain in the navy turning the corner ran and laid hold of him, "you rascal" said he "I've got one of you at last, I'll have you hung as sure as you are a man ;" Bryan implored forgiveness, "no, not 'till I see you at the yard arm," said the captain, "pray what ship do you belong to?" "the Tremendous sir," said Bryan, " why she is not on this station," said the captain, " yes she is sir," said Bryan, "she came the night before last," "Oh that may be" said the captain, " who commands her?" "captain Thunder sir," said Bryan, "the Tremendous, captain Thunder, why you d—d rascal you are making game of me, pray what's your name? " Walker," said Bryan, giving him a desperate blow under the ear which sent him sprawling, Bryan hastened to the boat, the others had arrived before him, he told the officers of his boat the whole affair, changed his dress and took his station as boat keeper, presently the captain came with his head on his hand, and a handkerchief under his ear, " muster all the pike men and flat boat men immediately," said the captain, 'twas done, they were mustered and all were present, the captain then walked by and looked earnestly at every man, at length he fixed upon Bryan, " what's your name?" said he, "Bryan sir," " are you sure it's not Walker?" said the captain, "no sir, my name is Paddy Bryan," "where have you been to day?" " I am boat keeper sir," when did you come on?" " at twelve o'clock yesterday," " and you have never left the boat?" " no sir," " where are the officers of this man's boat?" the lieutenant and midshipman answered, " here sir," " is this man boat keeper?" " yes sir," " has he never left the boat to day?" "no sir," "how do you know?" " because I have never left it myself," replied the Lieutenant, "why" said the captain " I caught a fellow killing a pig, and

I asked him what ship he belonged to, and he told me the Tremendous, I asked him who commanded her, and he said captain Thunder, and when I asked his name he said Walker, and gave me the dreadfullest poulter under the ear I ever received in my life, but the rascal has done me by G—d, I'd have hung him up like a rope of onions if I could have made him out, but he has done me, I can't help it;" he then went away.

Being (as I have hinted) hard put to it for provisions, I went one morniug with Baker captain of the Foretop down to the river, and observing a boat with various eatables for sale, we hailed her, but the Portuguese were afraid and kept off, we agreed to swim to and board her in the smoke, we did so, I boarded her on the quarter and Baker boarded her on the bows. Baker drew his cutlass and four great fellows in the boat fell on their faces, I threw a cheese on shore and half a keg of butter which was all we wanted, I swam to the shore put the cheese inside my jacket and marched off, leaving Baker to bring the butter, when he had left the boat, the Portuguese cried out " pillilu, ladaroon, &c." (meaning thieves) the Portuguese came running from all quarters, and we should have been butchered with their knives in a few minutes had not a party of English troops run to us to inquire what was the matter, I said " comrades we are fighting for these lousy vagabonds and they won't let us have a little cheese and butter to our biscuit," our troops began to show fight, knocking them down on all sides, they were very glad to get off.

One ship's company actually stole the church bell and sold it to a fellow in the creek. I set out in company with three others for a cruise about three miles from Alhandra, through orange groves, fig trees, limes, &c. The inhabitants were laying in groups by the hedge side, fields, or barns, having no home. We called at a place where a man had wine and auguadent to sell, after drinking pretty freely, I recommended two of them to walk off, a short time after I rose saying to my mate it was time to be moving, the man said, " de money John," I said "none care's the money" "none care's de money" said the fellow and running seized his sword and was about to strike, I struck him a severe blow across the hand with my stick and the sword fell to the ground, he then went to take down his gun, we both ran off, he fired after but missed us, alarmed as we were, we made shift to lay hold of some glass tumblers as we passed a booth where they were selling wine, with which we got clear off. Next night three of us agreed to make a push down to the French lines to get a belly full of wine, we set off and coming to our sentinel at the out post, entered into conversation with him about Yorkshire, &c., we seized our opportunity and ran towards the French, the sentinel presenting his piece, swore he would fire if we did not come back, we paid no attention, but got to the French tap, where the Frenchmen made us all drunk, and at midnight took us on there backs and by a circuitous round passed our sentry and left us in the road to Alhandra, we made shift to reach our quarters by seven o'clock, about eight next morning nearly eight hundred of us were drawn up, and ranked two and two, when an officer and a party of soldiers arrived having a prisoner with them, and the prisoner passing us said " my lads you have done a bad job for me." It appeared an officer had seen us run from this man the day before and concluded we had deserted to the enemy, he was relieved, tried and sentenced to recieve three hundred lashes, he was to be forgiven if he could pick out the men, this he could not do. The naval officer commanding the pike company said, " if the men were in the ranks, he would forgive them if they would step out and shew themselves," relying upon his honor I stepped out, and calling upon the other two they came out also, the man immediately recognised us and he was liberated, our captain gave us a slight reprimand and all was over.

We buried one of our men, he died of the flux, the Lieutenant read prayers in the Catholic Church, and I stood sexton and clerk, we buried him inside the Church, taking up some loose boards, we made a hole and putting him into an old corn chest interred him decently. I had much to do to get his jacket off as he lay dead; I sold it for nine shillings. Our men being much in want of slop clothing I made out a demand for them and sent the list to the ship, the slops were forwarded per order by the A. B. Transport, and I was sent to take charge of and give the master a receipt for them, when I saw the bale I suspected it had been plundered by the Transport's crew, I therefore refused to sign a receipt agreeable to invoice, unless I first opened the bale and counted the articles separately, this was agreed to when I found one third of the articles mentioned in the invoice wanting. I gave a receipt for what I actually received and issued them to the men as far as they would go, a number not getting their slops, wrote to the captain complaining of the same, the first Lieutenant thinking I had embezzled them, ordered me to be made a prisoner and sent on board, when I reached the ship, the first Lieutenant said, "so sir, I have got you at last have I." I told him I did not know what he meant, "Pray" said he "what have you done with the slop clothing which was sent to you for distribution?" I had an account in my pocket of the articles received and to whom delivered, this I tendered to him, referring him to the master of the Transport, who had the duplicate, after I explained to him the circumstance of the bale having been plundered and the precaution and circumspection with which I had acted, he commended my conduct, ordering me to go to his servant and get some grog. As Saul hunted David so did this man hunt me, but he never got the least advantage of me.

One morning a Lieutenant of the army passed hastily by, and hailing a Captain, said "I think we shall have broken heads for breakfast, for Wellington has given orders to skirmish as far as Villa Franca," "then" said the Captain, "it's time I had my breakfast," in less than ten minutes after I saw the same

Captain mounting and galloping towards Villa Franca. The French had retreated. I went to Villa Franca two days after and demanded provisions from the commissary. I saw the skeletons of several horses whose flesh had been cut off and eaten by the French soldiers, we were shortly after remanded to our ships. Our men had been long in the practice of selling their clothing, as they could get more for them from the Portuguese than they were charged to them on the ship's books. Our clothes were all marked with our respective numbers on the ship's books. One day slops having been served out to a great proportion of the ship's company, the first Lieutenant determined to try a scheme in order to detect any that might endeavour to sell their clothing, I had taken up a pair of blue trousers, which were marked 1010, my number; I went to one of the Gig's crew, and asked if he would give me six shillings for them and run all chances, he said he would, and took them, at night the Gig's crew were called away to go on shore for the Captain, when all were in the boat and ready to shove off, the first Lieutenant ordered a hand in the boat to hold her on, and the whole of the boat's crew were ordered up the side. The master at arms and ship's corporals were ordered into the boat to search for slops, when not less than an hundred articles were handed up the side and put under the sentry's charge till morning; my trousers were among them. I got a shipmate to sell me a pair, the waistband of which he had lined with cotton, when putting my number on in ink I put them in my bag

I was called next morning, the trousers were produced, and the first Lieutenant (with an infernal grin) said "I'll be damned if I have not got you at last," "me sir" "said I, very saintly," "Yes, you sir, and that I'll let you know, pray" said he "whose trousers are those"? " you can't get over this," I replied " I don't know sir," " You don't know by G—d but you shall know, what's your number on the ship's books?" "One thousand and ten sir." " And what number do you call this?" (pointing to the number on the trousers,) " One thousand and ten sir," "and dare you say they are not yours?" " they are not sir." " Nor never were?" "never sir," "nor you know nothing about them?" " Nothing whatever sir." " Where's the Captain's clerk, look over the slop issue list, and see if Brown took up a pair of blue trousers yesterday;" he looked, " yes sir." " Then where are your trousers, if these are not yours?" " Down in my bag sir," " Master at arms go down and bring his bag up, take care there's no chizzling;" he went and brought my bag, I turned every thing out of it, presented my trousers and told him I got them lined as soon as I took them from the Purser; he flew into a great rage, but at length said rather calmly, " I tell you what Brown, you are either a terrible scoundrel or a d—d clever fellow; but you have done me by G—d, but I can't help it."

I never witnessed a more disgusting scene than I did when on shore at Lisbon; perhaps not less than thirty or forty men of all ages were laid at their full length, in the public square, with their heads reclined on women's laps, who were taking the lice out of them and other parts of their bodies.

The characters of the Portuguese and Spaniards (as far as I have seen) are parallel,—they are indolent, filthy, and very treacherous. The buildings in the capital of Portugal are, with few exceptions, mere dung-hills compared with our clean cottages. The houses in Cadiz are much better in general, but nothing to boast of. The brass horse, in the square in Lisbon, is a piece of exquisite workmanship, there is a representation on its breast, of a ship, which report says once struck upon the Sand Bar going into the Bay, and that when boarded had nothing alive, save a dove upon its cat head.

A young man J. H. C. was once in the office on board the Barfleur with me, he had got into the victualling office here; on his hearing I was on board the Zealous, he came to see me and promised to get me a situation as ship's steward; a few days afterwards I was applied for and removed by an order from Vice-Admiral George Cranfield Berkeley, as steward of N. S. then bound for England—two able seamen being given in my room. In a few days we set sail for England, and after a pleasant voyage of six days, arrived safe at the anchorage at Spithead; after refitting and completing for sea we were ordered for Channel service, and our station was off Cherburg, Cane, Dieppe, &c. (the Sophia sloop of war was in company,) being a twenty gun ship, our complement was one hundred and fourteen men and boys. On arriving off Cherburg

Rear-Admiral Williams, telegraphed, "give me some hay or my cow will die,"—we sent him two bales. There were a great number of French fishing boats off Cherburg, and we frequently brought them to, and mutually exchanged fish for bread, beef, pork, &c.

Our Captain was the real *fag end of a vagabond*. I never sailed with so bad a fellow before nor since;—if tyranny and cowardice constitute a bad commander, I knew such a man.

The Captain of the Sophia soon put us into a better (or at least a different) way of getting fish, and we generally fired among the French boats and took a few out of each, but if any one attempted to run, we brought her to, and filled our boat from her, letting the others go free, a pilot for the coast was on board of us, his wife and family were at Cherburg, by his means our captain got a plentiful supply of vegetables, &c., the pilot contrived at last to get his wife and family on board, and he sent them to reside at Portsmouth. Having been out three months, and it blowing hard, we stood across channel; when near Beachy Head, about six in the morning, a French lugger privateer bore down upon us under easy sail; the captain came on deck, we cleared for action, but the keys of the magazine could not be found, and not a shot could we fire—all was cursing and confusion. The lugger was playing round and round us, firing musquets, &c., all this time the captain was dodging under the lee of the mizen mast, the lugger going athwart our bows. Ned

R. asked the captain if he would allow him to give her the stem, and run her down. "Oh no, oh no," said the captain, "perhaps she will strike;" it was obvious from his manner, that his backside was making buttons. The only gun that was fired was by *Jacobson*, a boatswain's mate; he filled a shovel with coals and threw them on the priming, she went off but did no execution. At length the Frenchman sheered off, and one of the crew stood on the ring tail and clapt his bottom at us. A galpin of a midshipman had the keys in his pocket and was walking the quarter deck all the time. I saw a Newspaper a few days after, and read the following,—" Observed His Majesty's ship, N. S. attacked by a French lugger privateer, which she beat off."

We again arrived at St. Helen's, and from thence to Spithead, my master obtained leave of absence for ten days to see his friends in Kent, unexpectedly we were ordered for sea and dropt down to St. Helen's, the captain sent for me ordering me to make a demand to complete the ship with provisions, I told him I could not as the number and content book was locked up in my master's cabin, and without it I could not tell the remains on board, he ordered me to write to my master immediately, and tell him to repair on board forthwith.

I instantly went to my desk and wrote as follows:— "Sir, I am commanded by Captain —— to request you will immediately join, the N. S. being ordered for sea."

I sealed it and took it on the quarter deck, ordering

the quarter master to send it on shore by the first conveyance, he promised to do so, this was at six in the evening and we were seven miles from Portsmouth; next morning at six I enquired if any boat had come to or left the ship, the answer was " No" at eight the Gig's crew were called away, upon hearing which I ran and requested the first Lieutenant to allow the coxswain to put my letter in the office, it being on service, he went and asked the captain leave, " Where is the steward?" said the captain, " Here sir," " What's the reason this letter did not go last night?" I replied, "no boat has been to or from the ship," He said "you and your master think to do as you please; put him in irons;" he went on shore, and returning in about two hours turned the hands up, ordered me to strip, and gave me twenty lashes.

I have given a fair and impartial account of the transaction and my reader may determine whether 1 have or have not proved the charge of cowardice and tyranny; my master returned shortly after to the ship, and assured me he was sorry to hear what had happened, as he was fully convinced I was not to blame, but that under circumstances he could not help it. Thus it is when power wantons in cruelty.

We resumed our station off Cherburg, and kept a good look out, understanding there was a French frigate lying in that harbour and only wanting cordage and men to fit her for sea: early one morning we interrupted a number of small craft creeping alongshore towards Cherburg, we sent two or three boats manned and armed to endeavour to cut them off from the land but the enemy coming down to the beach with their field pieces, the boats were recalled; a merchant brig ladened with timber and rope was deserted by her crew, and the wind being off the land, she came close under our stern, we lowered our boat, boarded and took possession of her and conveyed her to Portsmouth.

It was the captain's orders when at sea for me to place the key of the steward's room in the first Lieutenant's cabin, every day at two o'clock, this order I strictly complied with.

We were now ordered up the harbour and got lashed alongside the Cyclops Hulk.

I here obtained a week liberty, and went up to London to see my friends, it was seven or eight years since I had seen them, my father died whilst I was an apprentice at Sheffield; during my absence, our family connections had greatly increased, four of my brothers had married and all had children, more or less, the week expired (apparently) in less than no time, upon which I applied to the Admiralty to get my ticket renewed, there where perhaps no less than an hundred waiting for the same favor, an understrapper came to me and said very sternly "what I suppose you want liberty like all the rest?" I answered "yes," then said he "you may go about your business, for their lordships will grant none;" I had heard money spoke all languages, I therefore gave him a nudge, called him aside, and tipt him half a crown, his countenance changed, he spoke aloud "Oh are you the man that has applied three day's successively for liberty?" I said "yes," " stop there," said he, upon which he went upstairs to their lordships' apartments and in a minute called "William Brown, his lordship wants to speak to you." I was shewn to Sir Sidney Yorke's apartments, "Well" said his lordship " what is your reason for wanting longer liberty?" I told him on account of the great increase in my family connections I had not time to see half of them, he said " you don't want to *run*, do you?" I assured him not, then he wrote on the back of my ticket—" extend William Brown one week," and gave me a letter to the regulating Captain on Tower Hill, whose clerk demanded a shilling for writing to inform my Captain; my time being expired I rejoined my ship and had another cruise in the channel, from whence we again came to Spithead, while at this anchorage I was sent on board the Puissant, victualling ship, for provisions, I had never considered the order respecting returning the *key* (in harbour) as binding, consequently had never attended to it, it was in the forenoon and I had left the grog list with the serjeant of marines, and told him the *key* was hanging over the steward's room door, about ten or eleven o'clock the Captain's boat's crew were ordered to get their grog, the *key* could not be found, and the Captain ordered me to be put in the *report of prisoners*, it was afterwards found on the deck under the nail where I had hung it, upon my return I was informed the Captain had ordered me to be put in the **report**. I then determined he should not have the *brutal* satisfaction of making me a spread eagle again, if I could avoid it. In the evening he sent for me to know if I could go on shore in the morning, and fetch fresh beef and some vegetables for him, I told him I could, next morning being ordered and ready for sea, we got unmoored and hove one anchor up, the Captain then sent for me, telling me to go on shore for the beef, &c., I had packed up my clothes in bread bags, which I had taken for to hold the vegetables, we set off, a midshipman being in the boat, before we had left the ship five minutes I had the mortification to see the beef boat coming out to supply the fleet. The midshipman said "steward there's the beef boat, steer for her," I did so, got on board, and persuaded the *clerk*, (an old friend of mine,) to say they had no beef for us, upon which I wanted to go on shore, but the midshipman said, he would go on board first and acquaint the Captain; this was a damper to me, however upon going on board the Captain asked me, if I could procure beef on shore, " Yes sir," said I (though I knew better,) we went without a midshipman, and having got the vegetables, the beef wharf being (as I well knew) locked up, I followed the boat's crew to Sally Port, and ordered them to shove off, they asked me if I was not going on board, I said " no " upon which they all jumped out of the boat swearing they would be off too.

I remonstrated with them, telling them they belonged to a boat, and might avail themselves of another opportunity; I took them into the Rising Sun, and after treating them well saw them off to the ship, the boat was instantly hoisted up, they weighed anchor—and stood down channel, I set off to the half way houses, about two miles from Portsmouth, where I had a brother in law to whom I communicated my adventure; I got my whiskers off, and he furnished me with a suit of his long togs, (clothes) the same evening he gave the guard of the mail coach a guinea, who lent me his coat, which had at least a dozen capes on it, and I started for London.

I was somewhat afraid of the guard of soldiers at Post Down, having to drive through a gateway, the sentinel cried " halt," the coachman pulled up, he examined inside, and then looking at me said—"drive on," I thought this would do. There was another outside passenger in a plain surtout coat, and we got into conversation during the night, when I developed the whole of my scheme to him, but judge my surprise next morning early when changing horses, and being disposed for breakfast, we went into a private room, he took off the surtout, and I beheld a gold epaulette on his shoulder, observing my consternation, he said "don't be alarmed, you know my duty, but I will not hurt you, but admonish you to be careful to whom you disclose your secrets in future," he paid for my breakfast and a cheerer and we set off and arrived safe in London.

I was full of apprehensions and every man I met I thought was in quest of me.

I staid in London, and having had my frolic, I could not rest as I felt completely out of my element on shore.

Taking leave of my friends, I sailed down to Gravesend, and put up at the shoulder of mutton, being the rendezvous, after spending what money I had, I ran some shillings in debt, but got a remittance from London and paid off, I ran a second score of two or three pounds and then communicated my intention to Shephard master of the gang, to volunteer on board a man of war, after having previously made my will and power in favor of the publican, but I made it in the first name I could think of, so that he was not likely to recover much from me.

I was taken to the Captain of the gang, and he desiring me to write my name, I knew not what name to give myself, however I determined my name to be William Brown, which it was not, is not now, nor ever will be, what I mean to say is simply this, that as I made this addendum to my real name, for aught I know, it may serve as well as any other, nor am I confined to any particular name, having *four*, by which I am well known in various parts of England, as well as abroad, I just observe, that this place has been my residence for nearly twelve years and my real name is known to most, as it is written in my Sunday hat in legible characters, and the assumed name in my every day one.

I was sent to join the Stag frigate, Captain Phipps Hornby, I write his name in full, although as will appear in the sequel, he once touched me up in the bunt, and gave me three dozen lashes, notwithstanding he was as worthy a fellow as ever had command of a King's ship he did what every commander of a ship ought to do, he commanded his own ship; after a cruise off Rochfort, we captured after a long chase the Le Mae Lonease, french privateer of (I think) twenty guns, and one hundred and thirty men, also the Hebe schooner, from Philadelphia, bound to a port in France.

We were afterwards ordered home and refitted, we put into Falmouth, from whence we were to sail to the Cape of Good Hope with convoy.

The Stag's crew were most of them new raised men, Lord Mayor's Men, and the scrapings of Newgate; having a perfect knowledge of the signals, I was made signal man. I found on board her the same master as was master of the Triumph, the man who fought the duel at Gibraltar, he recognized me but had forgot my name. On my talking to him about the signal halyards and how I wished to have the swivels, &c., he said "have not you and I sailed together before?" I told him "yes," "in what ship?" I told him in the Triumph, he said it was so, when he saw my plan for the swivels, he said, "ah you learnt that from me, you can't do me," I said "I did once sir." "You did sir," said he, "how was that?" I told him "I drew a skin of quicksilver from between his legs in Cadiz Bay," "ah, d—n you" he replied "you are rascal enough for any thing of that kind."

A ship arrived in the offing, I observed her number and said it was the N. S., the Captain asked me how I knew, he looked at the signal book and found it so, I knew not what to do, for as signal man I was obliged to keep the deck all weathers, she came in and anchored within two cable lengths of us, I could distinguish every officer on board as they walked the deck, an hour after this turning round, I saw the *coward* and *tyrant*, on the quarter deck talking and walking with our Captain. I took a walk sideways like a crab, and when on the main deck the N. S's. boat's crew being on the gangway, I called them down shook hands, gave them some grog and we parted. I learnt from the coxswain they were bound to the West Indies, their complement was one hundred and fourteen men, and I have been since informed that only fourteen arrived alive in England.

A few days after we set sail with about five hundred vessels, the pleasantest sight my eyes ever beheld, under convoy of the Inconstant, &c., they were composed of the Mediterranean, East and West India, South American and other fleets of merchantmen, they rode majestic on the main. The Inconstant incessantly fired guns to make them take and keep their stations, when we made the Western Islands we completed our water at Madeira, anchoring in the roads. I got a few hours on shore and saw the Nunnery, &c.; from thence we sailed for our destination, when we reached the Equinoctial line, we went through the ancient custom of shaving the new comers, when or where this custom first originated is hard to determine. I take the liberty of giving the reader a brief sketch of the process; the launch being on the booms, was first filled with water, next a gun carriage, properly slung with ropes, was hoisted over the bows, and a voice, harsh and discordant, somewhat resembling distant thunder, was heard hailing the ship. "Board a ship a-hoy," "Hollo" replied our Captain, (from the quarter deck,) "What ship's that?" "The Stag," "Who commands her pray?" "Phipps Hornby." "Oh, if you please I wish to see my son's Captain," " by all means *Mr. Neptune.*"

Two bullocks' horns were blown and Neptune in his car with his trident appeared—this was Dick Lasey, a boatswain's mate, and an old seaman, on his being shipped on the forecastle, four men naked and blacked drew the car along the gangway to the quarter deck—his two black servants riding behind blowing their horns, upon stepping out, Neptune addressed the Captain as follows, " I hope Captain Hornby is well, I think I never had the pleasure of seeing you—nor your ship here before, the answer was no, which mulct the Captain of a gallon of rum for himself, and a gallon for the ship, Neptune and his attendants then proceeded to and took their seats in the boat—two who acted as barbers stood in the water with pieces of Iron hoops for razors.

The ship's company (with the exception of those who had crossed the line before,) were all confined down below and sentinels placed over the hatches, they were then called up one by one by the ship's books, upon their coming to the hatchway two men stood ready with a wet towel to blindfold them, they then asked " where do you come from?" when on attempting to answer their mouths were filled with filth, they were then conducted into the boat when they were well lathered with tar and something *much worse,* the barbers then applied their hoop razors and the blood followed the strokes, cries were altogether unheeded, and they were immersed overhead in the water, and kept there a short time; when the whole of the ship's crew were gone through, they began to throw the water taken out of the boat at each other indiscriminately, and all were equally free of the sea, this ended the ceremony.

When in latitude eight south, the Inconstant and other convoys parted company except the East India, which were then under our convoy, we succeeded in capturing a slave vessel having ninety slaves on board, they were laid on their backs in the hold, fastened to ring bolts in the deck, men women and children lay quite naked indiscriminately, they were nearly starved to death, the miserable wretch of a supercargo was an American, he had taken them from the River Gambia; being so far from any port we were under the necessity of letting them go.

I was much interested at observing the Albicore, Dolphin, and Bonetta, chasing the Squid or flying fish, in these seas ; I felt keenly for the fate of the latter as their enemies commanded two elements, when they rose out of the water to escape the jaws of the pursuers, they were equally in danger from the sea gulls and divers, which were watching their opportunity, the flying fish would spring for forty or fifty yards above the surface of the water, until their fins (or wings) losing their moisture, they fell like a stone, but would as suddenly emerge again.

We were ranked round the upper deck one Sunday morning all in white, when we were suddenly alarmed by a rustling noise resembling a hail storm, it was no other than a squad of flying fish that had either taken fright at the ship or were chased by other fish, they sprang on board and striking the backs of the men on the larboard side of the ship, completely spotted them like so many leopards, and the inky nature of the fluid was such, that it never could be got out again; as we neared the Cape, some cape Boobies as our men called them, perched upon our yards and were instantly asleep, the men went and took hold of them without their making the least attempt to escape, they somewhat resembled the goose, but the body was remarkably small, and their wings from tip to tip an amazing width.

At length we parted company with the convoy, and finally arrived at Simon's Bay, near the Cape of Good Hope, the harbour is landlocked, and perhaps a thousand men of war might find anchorage in it, the Bay also abounds in fish, of various kinds of which we partook largely, there is an English dock-yard at this place, and on going on shore I saw a man whipping a poor Negro who was naked and running with the hoop of a mast red hot. I found it was a boatswain with whom I had formerly sailed, I took the liberty of asking him how he could use a shred of nature upon the same common level with himself, in so inhuman a manner; he endeavoured to excuse himself by saying that such was the nature of these poor degraded beings, that if not kept under with the utmost rigour there would be no commanding them at all, a poor paltry subterfuge thought I, I could only add, God help them. I hope the condition of the Negroes is very different now to what it was then, surely the number of settlers from this country, together with missionary efforts, have produced a moral change in the conduct of the Dutch merchants and others at this place. The owners of slaves here had full liberty to punish their menials at pleasure, four men subsisted on the produce of whipping, their whips had very long lashes, and my shipmates saw a woman fastened to the ground on her belly, naked, her hands and legs were stretched to four iron bolts, the first man took the whip and standing at a distance took flesh at every stroke, to the number of twenty, the second and third did the same, when the poor creature said, "me do so no more," the mistress replied, " dat is vat I want to hear," she was then released after rubbing her back well with salt pickle; I have seen parties of those slaves on a Sunday, dancing round a piece of tin, which glittered in the sun, an old tin kettle served as a drum, and a bone as a drum stick.

We were dispatched from this place to Algoa Bay to inquire and endeavour to obtain information respecting the William Pitt, an extra ship taken up in the country, which had been missing for some time, we touched at and sent a boat on shore at Bird Island and saw some trifling remains of an Indiaman, (the Doddington,) which was wrecked on or near this Island; at Algoa there was an English Garrison, all we could learn from the Soldiers was, that a number of carcases of sheep and pigs, a hencoop, and the top of a medicine chest had come on shore; we got the top of the chest on which was cut out in deep and large letters "William Pitt," we concluded she must have foundered at sea.

There is a very dangerous place near Bird Island, a kind of whirlpool, which we skirted, had we been in the middle of it—it might have drawn us down; it stove in our quarter boat and did us other damage in an instant of time, happily for us we had a fresh breeze.

At the Roadstead where we dropt anchor, there was plenty of fish, but we could never put our lines down without getting hold of a shark, those voracious monsters will swallow any thing they see almost without exception.

A messmate of mine, after washing up the mess things, threw a table spoon overboard with the dirty water, four days afterwards a shark was caught alongside, and on opening him the spoon was found in its belly, this was in Simon's Bay, we had now returned to that place; four of our men deserted here and made their rugged way over the mountains to Cape Town, they got on board of a merchant vessel the Captain promising to secrete them, he however sent word on board a King's ship and they were taken and sent back to our ship.

We were dispatched from hence to St. Helena; the

Island where Bonaparte was confined, and where all his acquired glory is buried in eternal oblivion, as it respects himself, though in the page of history his name and his wonderful achievments will be handed down by the latest generations of time; I will not digress or certainly there is a field for reflection, which if indulged in, would fill a volume.

The Semiramis frigate was run aboard of by the Vansittart Indiaman, and being considerably damaged she was ordered to repair damages, and proceed to England with the Convoy instead of us, this we did not relish for we knew by experience "there is no place like home," we assisted in refitting and they set sail.

We got abundance of water cresses which grew in Lemon Valley, down the side of a very steep rock, watered by rivulets springing from every part of it, Ladder Hill presents a grand spectacle on entering the Bay, its amazing height with the flag staff at the top, seems to command respect.

I witnessed a curious sight while lying here, with the finny tribe. A Whale was attacked by the sword fish and thrasher. The former rose by a spring not less than twelve yards out of the water, and darting down, pierced the blubber of the whale which caused him to bleed profusely, the unwieldy bulk of the whale rendered it impossible to retaliate upon this bold intruder, the whale darted down but frequently rose to blow out of his spout holes; I was informed that the thrasher was equally active, diving deep and springing up endeavouring to rip open his bowels, this engagement was witnessed by the whalers on shore, who sent a boat and striking a harpoon into the whale, towed him ashore.

We returned from St. Helena to the Cape, we had a fine view of Table Land, but the anchorage at Cape Town is very dangerous; indeed ships are not allowed to anchor there in the winter or stormy months, the Union Jack being hoisted half mast high is the signal for ships to anchor in Simon's Bay, we shifted to the latter place, I was always partial to angling and I was never glutted with fish till this time; the sea around us was completely covered with fish of the mullet kind, and they seemed to want shelter from an enemy; they had been chased in by a vast quantity of large fish, which our men called cape cod; their weight was from twenty to thirty pounds each, they kept leaping out of the water seizing the small fish in their ponderous jaws; we took the small fish in great quantities, by lacing an iron hoop round a bread bag fastened to a rope; we flung it over the ship's side with the mouth downwards, and thus we enclosed a multitude of fishes, we also put one of the small fish on a hook, and throwing it out as far as we could, the cod instantly seized it; we had a caulker's stage alongside floating, on which about twenty of our men got with lines, and it was laughable to see the combat between the men and fish, for getting hold of a fish, it got foul of all the lines, and when the men succeeded so far as to get the fish on the stage, it would make such plunges that it would knock several off their legs and precipitate them into the sea, we got as many fish as would, had they been properly cured, have been sufficient for the whole ship's company all the passage home; after peppering and salting them we spread them on a small Island in the Bay called Sober Island, this name was given it by the Captain of the Lion, sixty four, the Armourer and mate of the Lion, had frequently been sent on shore to work, and as frequently returned drunk, the Captain contrived to erect his forge on this Island and called it Sober Island.

Unfortunately a wet season came on and our stock of fish was completely spoiled; this was the best full bellied station ever I was at, we got frequent supplies of mutton from the shore, and the fat of the cape sheep all running into their tails, (weighing from six to ten pounds each,) we found them superior to butter for frying fish, &c.

In our former passage to St. Helena, I should have mentioned we were only ten days running to that place, and no less than six weeks beating back again, this was owing to the trade winds always blowing in one direction, we took our final departure from this place having to touch again at St. Helena for convoy, on our passage one morning having to wash decks, (which we did every morning at four o'clock,) while stoning the quarter deck on our bare knees, I said to my comrades, " what do you say to a stave," they replied with all my heart, I then struck up and they joined me, the officer, soon silenced us, but I thought I would try again when I got on the gangway, being then off what sailors call, *holy ground*, we struck up again, but a midshipman was set to pick us out, and myself with three others were ordered aft prisoners; when the Captain came upon deck, the complaint was made by *Billy Eyeballs*. "Where is Mr. Brown and his disciples?" cried the Captain, I advanced with a face as long as a loin of veal and as white as a calf's head, " So sir you choose to make a noise in the execution of your duty, and with a degree of insolence to the officer of the watch; pray what was he singing ?" " why sir, it was twankadillo or some such nonsense." " Where's the boatswain's mate?" said the Captain, " here sir," " have you got your colt?" "yes sir," "then give Mr. Brown a good tickling for singing twankadillo," " aye, aye, sir."

I had buttoned my jacket ready and had laid a pair of pumps across my shoulders, he began to start away, I sang out blue murder although I never felt it. I said forgive me Captain if you please I'm always singing, I don't know when I sing and when I don't, that will do said the Captain; my disciples were three marines, the Captain therefore turned them over to their officer for punishment and during the three weeks we lay at St. Helena (after our arrival) they had to keep the deck four hours off and four hours on night and day. On arriving at St. Helena passing the N.W. battery they fired a shot over us, we knew not what to think concluding they must know the ship again having been there so recently, the Captain ordered the officer of the watch to carry on and take no notice, the battery then fired four shots at us which went between our masts we hove to and sent a boat to the battery to ascertain their reasons for firing at us, the officer commanding the fort said in reply that a few days previous, an American frigate, under English colours, had stood in, ranging alongside; a deep loaded East India ship fired a broad side into her when she hauled down the English and hoisted American colours, she stood out immediately under a press of sail and so great was the consternation of the officers and men, she was out of gun shot before they could give her a shot. In consequence of this he had received orders to bring every vessel to coming to this anchorage.

Prior to our leaving this place for England, we received intelligence that two American privateers were at the Island of Ascension watering. On our passage home we touched at this Island, sent a boat ashore and got some turtle, the boat returned and we went round the Island, firing shot on different parts of it, but no signs of any human being could be traced, we then continued our course.

I do not recollect any thing worthy of note from this time to the time of our arriving in England. The Stag frigate was a remarkable fast sailer but was very light built, on arriving at Portsmouth she was laid up and the ship's company draughted into the Spartan frigate, a larger and much stronger built vessel, our destination was for the Mediterranean. We took on board a number of deserters from the depot at the Isle of Wight, on arriving at Malta we took on board the Commander-in-Chief of the forces in the Mediterranean,

Sir Thomas Maitland, we visited and gave necessary instructions at the Ionian Islands; viz. Zante, Corfu, Cephalonia, &c. We touched at Palermo, Leghorn, Genoa, Marseilles, Toulon, Iris Bay, Syracuse, and a number of other places; I had often the gratification of seeing the Volcanoes Etna, Vesuvius, and Strombolo. Our ship lay in Naples mole near five months, I went on shore with some shipmates, we hired a carriage somewhat resembling a post chaise, and the driver being aware we wanted to see what we could, drove us by the Queen's Gardens, through the road cut through a solid rock at least a quarter of a mile in length, it was lighted over head with lamps, he then drove about four miles out to the Grotto del Cane, there is a large pond close by the grotto, an old man came out of a door-way having a dog tied to a band, he beckoned us and we went, he pointed to the cave and we observed a blue sulphur rising out of the earth about a foot high, he threw the dog in and in about four seconds the dog fell down, foamed at the mouth, and to all appearance died, the man drew him out and threw him on the grass where he lay for several minutes without the least sign of animation, the dog at length opened its eyes jumped about wagging its tail, and we patted it by way of congratulating it on its recovery, the old man by signs seemed to say, if a person should incautiously lay down to repose in the cave or grotto, it would be certain death. I mentioned the circumstance when I got on board and several of our officers resolved to go and see it, among the rest was Mr. B. the master, he insisted upon it it was an imposition of the man; they went and Mr. B. giving his watch to the first Lieutenant, said call me out when I have been in ten seconds if nothing happens, he went in and in four seconds fell to the ground senseless, the Lieutenant sprang in, seized him by the leg of his pantaloons and tore the leg off them, the party got him out and he lay senseless for several minutes, he at length recovered and rising up seemed as one awaked out of a deep sleep, he assured the officers he had never felt the least uneasy sensation.

Murat's horse at the Amphitheatre at Naples, is an exquisite proof of superior skill.

We lost a boatswain's mate here in the following manner, he went on shore in company with another seaman, and getting rather groggy acted rather imprudently with a woman in the public street, her husband was a corporal in the Neapolitan Guards, and was watching him, he came up to him drew his sword and cut him across the body so that his bowels came out, the assassin went to the Church put his finger in the key hole and his person was considered sacred, our Captain applied for redress to King Ferdinand and he promised the man should be punished. We went to sea and returning three months after, we learned that the man was set at liberty as soon as we left the Mole.

I was pleasingly struck with the conduct of four men, while we lay here, they were called divers; we had lost one of our anchors, and they came on board to recover it for us, two of them went down first in about seven fathoms water, they took a rope's end down with them, and succeeded in fastening it to the ring of the anchor, this done they came up, and the others sent a hawser messenger down the rope, and going down secured it, the time they were under the water might seem longer than it actually was, but I am of opinion they were at least three or four minutes.

It was at this place where I got served out by Captain Phipps Hornby, I had been on shore on liberty, and fearing my cash would not hold out had put a pair of good blue trousers on under my white ones to be ready for sale in case of necessity; I sold them to a Neapolitan, as several of my shipmates had sold to the same man, like a blockhead he had hung them at the door to expose them for sale, the numbers were full in view, and our worthy Captain having four eyes saw them, and judging they had belonged to his men took the numbers down, and on coming on board ordered the drummer to beat to divisions every man bringing his bag, they were severally examined by the division list, every officer having an exact account of his men's clothing, we were taken by surprise and could not do as we had been accustomed to do, which was to throw shoes and other articles across the deck to each other; that is suppose my clothes had beed examined I then handed or threw shoes, stockings, &c., to any that were short; I was at this time ship's corporal and my clothes were never mustered, I therefore did as usual, lent my apparel all over the ship, the officers not paying so much attention to numbers as to the complement, on this occasion however I was ordered to bring my chest up, the Captain having discovered my number on the trousers. In vain I pretended I had lost the key of the chest, the Armourer was ordered to pick the lock, on doing which it was found to be full of emptiness; on being asked where my clothes were, I said they would be forthcoming in an hour's time, with the exception of the trousers which I admitted I had sold. I would never disclose who I had lent my things to, or I might have fared better, but a number of my shipmates would have shared the same fate as myself, I got my three dozen and all was over.

It is a trait in a seaman's character never to sell or split one of another, but in one instance this standing rule was reversed, as I forgot to mention it in its proper place I insert it here. It happened on board the *Glory;* the only townsman I had on board was James Green, a cutler from Sheffield, we had been drinking some wine together and as he had the first watch on deck, he answered his muster at *one bell* or half past eight, and instead of keeping the deck until twelve he went below to his hammock, about eleven the officer mustered the watch again, Green was missing, the boatswain's mate was sent below in search, he came up again, saying he was drunk in his hammock, in the morning he was reported, the first Lieutenant sent for him on the quarter deck, and said if he would tell where he got the liquor he got drunk with, he would forgive him, he said Brown the ship's corporal bought it for him, a messenger came down below and told me Mr. L. M. wanted me on the quarter deck, I asked him *what was up*, he said *Green* was there and had said something about me buying wine; I went, "pray" said the first Lieutenant "where did you get the wine you made this man drunk with?" "why" said I "it's no use making things worse by telling a lie, I bought him a bottle," "who did you buy it of?" I replied "I was groggy myself and could not tell," (had I told, the seller would have been flogged as well as myself,) he said he would make me tell; at seven bells the hands were turned up to punishment, and once more I had to feel the lash, which by the bye is no trifle; the Captain addressing himself to *Green* said "Mr. *Green*, I have had the honor to command a King's ship twenty eight years, and never before knew an instance of a man disclosing a secret to the injury of another, however" said he "as Mr. L. M. promised to forgive you, you are forgiven, take care of yourself." After this he got monkey's allowance, more kicks than half-pence; a few days after an officer reported him for insolence, he was seized up and received my complement of *three dozen*.

We had received intelligence of peace, and expected to be ordered home every week. On receiving orders to that effect we reconnoitered Algiers, touched at Gibraltar, and set sail for England.

On arriving at Portsmouth we were ordered to be paid off and a few days after the Ajax, 74, and Spartan frigate were paid off accordingly. I landed at Gosport and was joined by nine of my shipmates, we could not get a coach to convey us to London, we therefore agreed to hire a fish cart, agreeing to pay the man one pound each. We now agreed to keep quite sober as there was no more piping to grog or meat, and to ensure this we took three cheerers each, and not wishing to be detained on the road, we also took ten bottles of rum in the cart. I never recollected what happened after starting, till two days after I awoke and found myself in an elegant room at Charing Cross, London. I rang the bell the waiter came, I asked him if I was not at Charing Cross, he said " yes," I asked him how I came there, he said " I came the day before much intoxicated that I staid till night, and they thought it was a pity to turn me out, they therefore put me to bed." I felt my pockets but could not find a penny, though I had received upwards of twenty one pounds two days previous.

I asked the waiter if he had got my money, "no" said he " you were giving your money and liquor away very freely." I began to reflect it was many years since I had seen my friends and was now coming among them pennyless—I was putting on my trousers, when pulling up the waistband something like paper cracked under my thumb, I found the lining ript, and on putting in my finger pulled out a five pound and a two pound note, I rang the bell and the waiter came, " what's good for a sore head?" said I, " a bottle of ginger beer for your life" said he, "go you dog and fetch it there's life in a Muscle yet," he brought it and I paid him two shillings for it and left the house, after giving him two shillings for himself. I then went to see my mother she was very feeble, having attained her seventy third year; I had the happiness to find the family in general in a prosperous way.

I wrote to Mr. M. at Sheffield, with whom I had been apprenticed, offering to serve the remainder of my time on reasonable terms, if he was in want of an assistant; he wrote to say he was not in immediate want, but wished me not to make any permanent engagement as he might want me shortly, he also requested me to purchase some articles to the amount of four pounds twelve shillings, to send them, and he would remit me my money by return of post, (I had lost all my clothes in the *fish cart* except a new suit I had on,) I sent as requested, but receiving no letter or money, I wrote to Mr. M. again—my little stock of money being exhausted, I resolved to offer my services again in His Majesty's service.

I went on board the Tender at the tower, but my fingers were an objection, they would not receive me; my spirit was always bigger than my purse, and I resolved not to go near my friends circumstanced as I was.

Sheffield was my parish, and although I had but four-pence in the world, I resolved to set off on foot; the distance from London is one hundred and sixty three miles, and on my reaching that place I might recover the sum I had advanced for Mr. M. and get employment in my own business; I set off the latter end of the year 1816, being on the Barnet road I was hailed by a post chaise driver, who asked me if I would ride, I told him I had no *possibles,* "jump up" said he " I know you sailors are hearty chaps when you have" I rode with him to Barnet and got lodgings at the house where we stopped; I had beside the copper a French shilling, I gave it and two-pence for my lodging, I had then two-pence left, after buying a penny roll and a penny-worth of cheese, I set off and walked several miles ruminating on my fate, at length overcome with fatigue and hunger, I found there was nothing for it but begging, I made up to several fine buildings but my heart failed me and I wandered into the road again, at length hungry and thirsty my soul fainted within me. I saw an elderly lady walking through a meadow, I stepped up to her and craved her charity, she said she had no change, thank you said I all the same as if you had, I had not gone many yards before I heard her call out " here stranger" when going up to her she said " you don't seem like a person that is used to begging here's a shilling for you."

Reader, judge my feelings, this was the first time I ever asked alms of any one, and if ever I prayed fervently, it was then, that heaven would reward her liberality in both worlds; I set off determining I would travel as far as possible with this shilling.

Arriving near Northampton I fell in with a man who had an apron on, on our entering into conversation I found he was one of my present profession, he began to relate how fortune had favoured him in this way, and told me if I would join him, I might live like a gentleman, and he would travel my road; this was too good an offer to be refused, when we got to Northampton I furnished him with a paper representing him as a cordwainer out of employ, having a wife and eight children to support. The inhabitants of that place are principally shoemakers, we put up at the Three Cups, and with this paper he went round to the trade, subscriptions were made for him in every shop; meanwhile I called upon Lord Spencer, Sir Philip Bouverie, and others, making ends meet well.

We lived on the best and, remained here three weeks; at last thinking our stock was exhausted we set off again, we had not travelled above two miles when passing the Hare and Hounds, my partner said to me, "let's go in and get some rump steaks and oyster sauce," I told him we must raise the wind first, upon which he said, "Bill you are a good fellow, I have tried you all ways, look here," when putting his hand into his pocket he pulled out a handful of silver, we went in and called for beef steaks, porter, &c. the landlady was a shy old dame, but upon my comrade's jingling the silver in his pocket, her countenance changed and she modestly replied, they will be ready in a few minutes; we seldom travelled above four miles a day and considered it bad work if we fell short of five shillings each, my partner however absconded without leave, and I fell in with a *sham* sailor. I have witnessed some strange things at different lodging houses, soldiers who never handled a musquet, sailors who never saw a sea-port, men with one leg who had two as good legs as mine were, and others who *merely pretended* to have lost an arm. Some upon what is called the high fly. These are respectable in their dress and appearance and can produce documents which fail not to deceive the well disposed; as for instance,—A man is represented as having been Captain of the Good ship Rover, from Liverpool, bound to America, but was driven through stress of weather ashore on the coast of Ireland, where it was with the greatest difficulty the crew were saved, the vessel went to pieces and the cargo was completely lost; we therefore recommend A.B. Captain of the said ship to the consideration of a generous and humane public. Then follows a list of subscribers, of one pound, five pounds, &c., the above *sham* Certificate is also signed by the mayor of Dublin, &c. &c. Here follows a N.B. No part of the ship or cargo was insured.

We came to a public house in a country village, where a young man and an old farmer were differing, I told the former he should not quarrel with one old enough to be his father, he said, "do you take it up?" I said "yes I do." I told the old gentleman to back me for a guinea and I would soon shew him how it was done, the farmer backed me, the young man accepted the challenge, and the two guineas were posted in the Landlord's hands. I whispered to my antagonist, we would have a sham fight, to which he consented, we set to and I *pretended* to give him a heavy body blow, in the next round he gave me a blow under the jugular, I sprang backward, put my head through a pane of glass, and said he was too heavy for me; I gave in, the old man cursed and swore, give me my horse, thieves, murder, he got on his horse and set off full gallop crying out murder. We sat down and drank the old man's guinea together.

We were now joined by another an American seaman, and coming down the hill leading to Nottingham, I made up to a gentleman in a gig, " will you honor help an old sea dog in distress, smither my timbers," said I, "it's a lubberly trick to be cut down to the water's edge." " What are you?" I replied " a seaman." " What ship?" upon which I began to name the whole of the ships I had sailed in—" Why," said he, " you have been in the whole fleet." " Please your honor just drop a trifle under your lee and I'll step into your wake and pick it up," he put his hand into his pocket and flung down a three shillings piece, " I give you that" said he, " because I belong to the navy myself." " God bless your honor," I rejoined, " I hope your boots will never spring a leak." " Go to hell you son of a b——," I walked off.

When we got to Nottingham we waited at the Town-hall for relief, the Mayor sent out four pence, but on my giving the constable to understand there were three of us, he said if he went in again the Mayor would be raving mad, I urged my point, he went in and the old fellow was out in a trice, where are those rascals—which of these fellows got the four-pence, I was not willing to part with it, and I told him I had nothing to do with the other two, but he insisted upon my giving it, he gave me a shilling in exchange, ordering us out of the town immediately.

We next came to Loughborough, and waited upon the constable for relief, he was not at home, and his wife refused to give us any thing, saying there were two sailors there for relief a week before, and on searching their pockets they found two shillings upon them, and they were committed to the House of Correction; I took the hint being cash keeper and kept outside the door, she searched the other two, but could give them nothing, upon their coming out we agreed to stand against the shop window till she gave us something, a number of people gathered round us and collected about five shillings for us, upon the woman seeing us stop she called me and gave me a shilling; we went to a public house opposite and sent her shilling back with another to buy some beef steaks, and (the constable was a butcher,) we had a merry night together.

In the morning drawing near to Sheffield, I parted with my two companions, sharing about ten shillings each; upon my arrival I went to my late master and after taking some refreshment demanded the money I had advanced for him in London, which he paid me: I purchased some wearing apparel and waited upon some pawnbrokers, but trade was so excessively dead they had scarcely any employment for the hands they then had, I knew not what to do, but passed the time while my money lasted with my old associates, ringers, singers, &c.; at length my fund was done and getting shaved, a Mr. F. was telling the barber he wanted a hand to make a trench and a fence in a garden, I offered my services, which he accepted, and furnishing me with tools I went to work, the fence was a quickset and having no mittens I found it an awkward job, but I made them stand one against another somehow. I went and got my wages, nine and sixpence, but I am of opinion had there come a very moderate breeze of wind, all my work would have to be done over again.

I was one evening in Water Lane, and a person, (judging my circumstances,) called me into a private room, and told me it was a pity to see such an one as me destitute, and that he could put me in a way which would make me a gentleman, I thought I could have no reasonable objection to his proposal, and assuring me it was an honest calling I agreed with him.

We set off together and I soon found it indispensably necessary to have recourse to *cadging*. I scarcely know how many towns and villages he led me through, nor do I remember their names, but I discovered he had a knack that I was unacquainted with, he visited minister's and gentlemen's houses, under pretence that his wife had fallen in labour in a neighbouring village; by this means he acquired a quantity of linen shirts, shifts, sheets, &c, and money in addition, he let me see the grand secret at length which was to make my fortune, they were two pieces of canvas painted over, and the several sums of sixty guineas, &c., down to a crown, on various parts of the canvas, the betters laid down a shilling each on what number they pleased, every sum having a number attached to it; they were then to throw two dice in a box, which were so constructed that it was impossible to throw a winning number, it is true in counting the dice he would sometimes make a *pretended mistake* in counting and award a crown, but this was to give the bystanders a keener edge; he never practised the jokes (as he called them,) but at fairs, races, &c.

On arriving at Catterick he borrowed a table and went on the race course and trade was very flush, I wanted (as he promised,) one of the jokes, but he wished to have all to himself; I counted upwards of three pounds which he cleared the first day.

On our way home to our lodging, I asked him how he had come on, he said "faith very badly, I have not got salt to our porridge" I past it off quietly; the next day we went again and getting no employ myself, observing some men setting up sticks and putting half-pence upon them, I thought I would try the same scheme which I did, and in about two hours cleared four shillings, I thought if this trade had lasted for ever it would have done.

The races were over and we returned again to our lodging at Catterick, he still complained he had taken nothing, when I went to bed, I told the woman who kept the lodging house, if he did not pay for us both, I would pay my own, but to get it of him if she could. In the morning early she called me out of bed saying he had just slipt off, he had paid half and left me to pay the other, I ran down the town after him and caught him, he in vain pretended he was coming back again, I told him to give me as much as would pay the woman, and I never wished to see him again;

in spite of all I could say he would give me nothing, I gave him a good thrashing and he pulled out a knife and threatened to stab me, I knocked him down, took the knife from him and then left him. I paid the woman and hearing the women and men lodgers talking of Middleham Moor, I thought as the races were the week following I would go, I had never been in the North of England before, I got to this place, and knew not until two hours after but what I was at Leyburn, I attended the races and cleared a few shillings; I felt completely tired of this line of life, and entering into conversation with my landlord, I repeated some of my travels to him, on my mentioning that I had sailed with Sir John Orde, he interrupted me by saying that a nephew of his, the Honorable T. Orde Powlett, lived within three miles of this place, and that he was now at the head Inn. I wrote a few lines mentioning my services and requesting relief, receiving no answer I went to Bolton Hall, (his residence,) and saw him in company with Lord Orde (as I was afterwards informed,) walking before the Hall, I stepped up to him and informed him I was the man that took the liberty of writing to him. " Oh," said his honor, " you sailed with Sir John Orde, did you?" " yes Your honor," " Sir John's dead," " I am sorry to hear it," " Yes he's dead, and I know nothing about it." " I sailed with him from Spithead the 1st of November, 1804, your honor," "I know nothing about it" was the reply; I saw the Honorable Captain Dundas at Catterick, and he said the respect you bear to the memory of Sir John should induce you to help an old servant of his, he still remained inexorable. "Your honor" said I "John Lisle Coulson was his flag Lieutenant," upon hearing this he called, "Orde, was Coulson Sir John's flag Lieutenant?" "Yes he was," then turning to a farmer looking man that followed he asked him if he had any silver; the man replied, "Yes sir," "give this man five shillings" said he, I received it thankfully.

When I left my lodging at Middleham, I told them if I got any thing I would return, if not, I should never see them again, upon receiving this weighty *sum*, I determined if possible to lay the foundation of my future happiness, should any opportunity offer. I returned to Middleham, mentioned my success, and said if I could get a few children to teach I would never travel more, old Peggy, my landlady, said " if you begin I'll uphold it you will get forty scholars, poor people's *baines* can get no *larning*," from my recollection of the charitable disposition of the Methodists, I inquired if there were any of that denomination there, "Aye, marry is there" said old Peggy, " and there be one over the way that's a *rait un*." I wrote a few lines to Mr. Christopher Simpson, opening my mind most freely, giving him a reference to my friends in London, and requesting his friendly interference to recall a wanderer to society and to the paths of virtue. I mentioned my thoughts of teaching, &c.

It is wholly unnecessary and superfluous for me to point out the excellencies of this worthy man, to say the least of him, he was a Bible Christian in the fullest and strictest sense of the word, and take him for all in all I never shall see his like again; Shakspeare says " shew me the man that is not passion's slave, and I will bear him in my heart, yea in my heart of hearts, yea in my heart's core," had the tragedian lived in Christopher Simpson's days, I should not have hesitated to have held him up with unbounded confidence, but alas! my friend and benefactor is gone to his reward and his works have followed him.

No sooner did he receive my letter than he came directly in person, "Where" said he "is the man?" when on casting his eyes towards me, " Come" said he " you are the man I want, you must come with me." I followed him to his hospitable mansion, was seated at his table with the family and satisfied my hunger with good things, indeed the whole seemed interested in my welfare, being a numerous family, Mr. C. S. encouraged me in my intended project, and my landlady offered me the small lodging room to commence with; embracing this offer I wrote my terms, and published them at the market cross. I got a board and painted on it a Day School by William Brown, I placed this board in the window, I lay on a chaff bed on the floor having no bedstead; I had a board by the side, and another at the bottom, to prevent my rolling off.

I got some sticks and boring some holes in the boards they served for forms by day, and finding a piece of a broken spoon it served as a pencil, one of the form legs supplying the want of a ruler.

I soon got scholars to the number of sixteen.

Matthew Atkinson, my landlord, was taken suddenly ill, and his sickness terminated in death, he was a harmless inoffensive man, his *rib* Peggy, was *what she was,* " when you speak of the dead tread lightly over their graves."

A few days previous to M. A——'s death his wife turned me and my scholars into the street, the only reason she assigned was, " she had known *mony* a *mon* that *coudn't dee* quietly where there was *sike* a noise."

Mr. C. S. conducted me to an empty house belonging to a relation of his, telling me to remain there till I could mend myself, in this I continued between eight and nine years, and am still under the same landlord.

My number of scholars has often exceeded the predicted number of forty.

It was in June, 1817, when I entered the former house, I had not been in it many days when I received a letter from Mr. C. the resident curate of this place, charging me to desist from teaching, or quit the place; I now concluded all was over, I thought the Almighty had fixed his fiat against me.

Mr. C. grounded his charge on my not having a license to teach, that he was spiritual guide of Middleham, and urging the impropriety of his allowing a person to teach of whom he knew nothing, and had no reference as to character, &c., I replied, and several letters were exchanged which are with their answers, in the possession of a brother of mine in London, (if not lost or destroyed,) application for which I have recently made.

I was like a man drowning who is ready to catch at a straw.

I was not willing to give up my point; eighteen householders signed a petition, addressed to the neighbouring magistrates requesting I might be allowed to continue, they gave me every encouragement so to do. There was a sentence in one of Mr. C——'s letters which I conceived was predominant. It was as follows " I understand you have been upwards of two months in this town, and I have never once seen you at Church;" allow me to give very briefly, my sentiments on this head.

I profess then to be a lover of the Church, I was brought up to nothing else, my parents were (read page 5th,) decidedly so, her prayers homilies, &c., are not to be excelled, but I claim to myself that liberty I most readily grant to others, the liberty of worshipping God in that way which is most congenial to my own feelings, admitting such mode of Worship be consistent with the revealed word and will of himself; I can attend any stated ordinance of public worship, without being tight laced, or imbibing principles which I may conceive to be repugnant to that sacred revelation from heaven with which we are so highly favored; this I claim as my birth-right as a rational intelligent and responsible being; this liberty is granted by the just and equitable laws of my Country, and I now appeal to men of candour, whether I can reasonably be thought blameworthy, if I have felt a peculiar attachment to the body of Christians called

Methodists, of these I may with the utmost propriety say, " I was naked and ye clothed me, hungry and ye fed me, sick of sin and ye visited me, in the prison of unbelief and ye opened mine eyes to behold wonderous things in the law of God ;" yes, I assert it, " Methodists with all your faults I love you still," and I ask what church miltiant is without spot and blameless, I never expect to see the desirable sight, till by grace 1 am called to behold the Church triumphant above.

As it respects myself, my greatest grief of mind is, that I have been a disgrace rather than a credit to that community. I can assign but one reason, and the reader may find the sum total in St. Paul's seventh Chapter to the Romans, concluding with these words (more appropriate cannot be) " O wretched man that I am ; who shall deliver me from the body of this death ?" Allow me to add, I have always found a life of piety and devotedness to God, the best (nay I may say) the only happy life.

I have but one hope and that is, my practice and my principles being constantly at war with each other, the latter may eventually overcome the other.

But to resume my narrative, my final letter from Mr. C. allowed me three months to leave the town, or give up teaching, at the end of which period he would punish me with fine and imprisonment, if I persisted.

I knew not what to do, but a friend relieved me from this dilemma, it was an act of mercy, wholly disinterested, as I had never seen the individual before;

he asked if Mr. C. was not troubling me; I said, Yes; he said, it was a shame, and putting his hand into his pocket presented me with the following lines, 24th of George Third:—"Any person having been in His Majesty's Navy or Army, since his accession to the Throne, shall be liable to set up in any town in England, (with the exception of the Universities of Cambridge and Oxford,) Ireland, or Scotland, and follow such trade, calling, or occupation as he is fit and capable for, and any person molesting or attempting to molest such person by means of using such trade, &c., shall be fined, with double costs." Put that, said he, in your pocket, and take no further notice. I did so, and never heard any more of this matter.

I have now arrived at the age of 46, I continue my School, which I have attended here near twelve years. I conclude with my warmest thanks to those who have entrusted their children to my care, requesting a continuance of their favours.

I am, reader, thy well-wisher,

WILLIAM BROWN.

I subjoin a few lines of poetry, wrote by me at sundry times.

The following lines were written on the occasion of John Breare, Esq. presenting to the Church six new Bells—wrote on the day they were *first rung;* *my boys manifesting the greatest desire to hear them.*

What sound strikes the ear,—one, two, three, four, five, six,
'Tis music's sweet charms the attention does fix;
In vain I endeavour to make boys do well,
No attraction can turn from the sound of the bell.

Well, if you so incline, I have nothing to say,
Command, and the youngsters shall have holiday;
When you're gone, they'll remember and drop the big tear,
O'er the memory so sacred of Mr. John Breare.

That home is sweet, alas! 'twill ne'er be mine,
Absent from that, an abject wretch I pine,
To long, to pant, to ardently desire,
A mortal's love, immortal only higher
In his esteem, for *Delia* has such charms,
The lover's only home—is in her arms.

Brown's sweet Home.

Written on being admonished to "Keep within bounds."

Can'st thou set bounds to love, hast thou that art,
To allay the writhings of a conquered heart,
Conquer'd by love, sure 'tis a deadly wound,
In life, in death, that never can be bound.

Written on purchasing the image of a Cock, and placed as a label to its Breast.

Chanticleer's voice struck Peter to the heart,
When godly sorrow, pleasing, painful smart,
Possess'd the coward who denied his Lord,
But kind upbraiding looks him straight restor'd.
Oh! through those clouds of darkness, may I see
Mercy's bright beams, and weeping bitterly,
Become as Peter, valiant for my God,—
Ere he take vengeance with his iron rod.

W. B.

I.

Esau repentance sought, but sought too late,
How many Esaus since have shar'd his fate;
Learn then that he, who oft reprov'd has been,
And harden'd still his heart, committing sin
With greediness, shall fall to rise no more,
Beyond all other, his damnation's sure.

II.

What then remains, while he continues here,
But to fill up his measure without fear,
Regardless of th' Almighty's vengeful ire,
To rush 'midst fiends and Devils to hell fire,
There joining chorus, make old Tophet ring,
And looking upward, curse his God and King.

W. B.

I.

I have a wish, doth ev'ry wish excel,
I wish to know, to feel the pains of Hell;
Then starting back to life, rush through the air,
Gaze into Heav'n, and view the contrast there.
'Tis true, I, Moses, and the Prophets have,
If I believe not these,—Christ cannot save.

II.

O faith, thou gift of Deity, descend,
My unbelief and misery to end,
Till then ne'er let the mighty struggle cease,
Till all this mighty stir within be peace.

Brown's Wish.

"Come thou with us and we will do thee good," &c.—April, 1828.

COME; or, *Brailsford's Invitation.*

How pleasing to the ear, most welcome sound,
Echo the note to all the nations round,
Tell Jew and Gentile, savages or tame,
There's life, and health, and peace in Jesu's name.

Come vilest reptile of the human race,
Come and partake of free, of sov'reign grace,
Come conscious sinner, come and prostrate fall,
Come give up all for him, who died for all.

Hark, 'tis the messenger of peace invites,
Come hungry soul, come feast on his delights,
His bleeding heart and hands invite you, come,
My message is, in Christ there still is room.

However black with crime or stain'd with blood,
The Saviour cries, "I bore thy heavy load,
Thy sins were nail'd to th' accursed tree,
Haste troubled soul and find thy rest in me."

W. B.

Friends, should you feel a glow of heavenly fire,
Remember him whose unstrung harp, lute, lyre,
Hangs on the willows, who in spirit groans,
And deeply conscious of his folly moans.
Oh, bear him in your faithful prayers to heaven,
So shall the brand be pluck'd, the wretch forgiven;
God will applaud the act, he will approve,
And through eternity reward your love.

W. B.

SUPPLEMENT.

Having in the foregoing pages given an outline of my narrative, for it is nothing more; having written the whole from memory, and within the last three weeks, besides attending my school business, it will not be wondered at, that I have omitted many circumstances which I should have recorded; however, upon a perusal, I find nothing recorded but what is strictly correct, and the omissions so far as I can recollect them, shall be inserted here, promising should any thing worthy of note hereafter strike me, to insert it, in the event of a second edition being called for.

On the subject of Religion I have been almost silent, as I concluded the pious mind would revolt at seeing such a continued scene of inconsistency in one frequently under the strivings of the spirit of God, one who has rejoiced in a sense of pardoning mercy, and (strange as it may appear,) one who has been employed in calling sinners to repentance, here I would exclaim? "Tell it not in Gath," &c. When I reflect on these things my soul chooses strangling rather than life; one thing I feel thankful for, that is, I never gloried in my shame; you will be ready to inquire how can this be, what can be the cause? I answer, first an undue attachment to liquor, this I acquired on board of ship, being steward, and having charge of the liquor, I frequently put a thief in my mouth to steal away my brains, and such is the force of habit, that though there may seem to be a complete mastery gained over this or any other easily besetting sin, and the individual may conclude the enemy he has seen to-day he will see no more for ever; yet in an evil and an unguarded moment, the enemy of souls may come in as a flood, Sampson may be shorn of his strength and become weak like another man, "yea, the last state of that man will be worse than the first."

> In opposition to the Calvanistic creed,
>
> " Ah, Lord, with trembling, I confess
> A gracious soul may fall from grace,
> The salt may lose its seasoning power,
> And never, never, find it more."

As this may be the most profitable part of my writings as it relates to soul matters, I will without any reserve relate my experience of divine things simply as it has been.

I mentioned my attachment in early life to the Bible; this attachment I never lost, and when a mendicant, carried my bible with me. It was about my nineteenth year, when I felt strong conviction of sin, of righteousness, and judgment; I saw myself in the gall of bitterness, and in the bonds of iniquity; I envied the happiness of those who professed to feel an interest in the Redeemer's blood, I attended every means of Grace, and was given to see the plan of salvation as revealed in the Gospel, my burden increased and became intolerable. I joined the society called Methodists, but was not joined to Christ by living faith, but my language was "Restless, resigned for thee I wait, for thee my vehement soul stands still."

Mr. Wesley's Hymns were (next to the bible) my sweets, amid those bitters.

I was very conscientious in relating the exercises of my mind through the week to my class leader, Mr Beat, just as they were; these were without exception the most useful means I ever attended. I gave my assistance to the Sunday School.

At this time Mr. W. E. Miller was at Sheffield, and many were the seals to his ministry. I went every evening when he was in town and resided in Carver Street, and stood outside his door to hear him pray with his family. It was not until I met with the disappointment from Mr. R. and joined Mr. B. that I was clear of my acceptance with God. I give the statement as in the presence of him who is to be the judge of quick and dead. I returned home one evening from a meeting and felt the arrows of the Almighty to stick fast in me, on retiring alone to my bed room I knelt down and wrestled in prayer, till in an agony, my language was, "If I never find the sacred road, I'll perish crying out for God." I felt

"The pleasing pain, the anxious smart,
"The meltings of a broken heart."

My thoughts then turned and fixed on the blood of Christ by faith; I beheld him extended on the cross, I saw the soldier, the spear, the wound inflicted, and the blood and water gushing therefrom;—at this moment I found him whom my soul desired to love,—the healing balm was applied,—the room seemed to blaze with light, and a deep impression of the following words was made on my mind, "Thy sins which were many, are all forgiven thee, rise and sin no more."— My chains instantly fell off, my heart was free, I arose and followed him who had thus manifested his love to the chief of sinners.

On reading this part of my narrative, some may be disposed to cavil, others to scoff, some may call it enthusiasm, fanaticism, &c. but I speak the words of truth and soberness,—my conscience also bearing me witness in the Holy Ghost; I am therefore the less careful in this matter. Previous to this manifestation, I was lame, blind, and dead—lame in all my mental faculties, blind to all spiritual things, and dead in trespasses and sins.

Prior to this mighty change, I never opened the sacred treasury of God's word, but I wrote bitter things against myself; the threatenings were mine,—an angry

God, an approaching judgment, and a yawning hell. But the scene was reversed: God reconciled, promises mine, Heaven in prospect, judgment welcomed, hell defied; I went on leaning on my beloved, and could then sing with the poet, " the winter's night and summer's day glide imperceptibly away, too short to sing thy praise."

I rose with the lark, heard its melodious notes, " Sweet is the breath of morn, her rising sweet with songs of earliest birds,"—every plant, every leaf, every flower, in a word, all things in nature led up to nature's God; during the business of the day, prayer and praise sat upon my tongue, pious breathings, holy inspirations, then enabled me to sit " calm on tumult's wheel;" my thoughts constantly soared above the scanty bounds of time and space, and my soul longed to breathe a purer air; my delight was with the excellent of the earth, and with such as excelled in virtue. I thought my hill so strong that nothing could shake it, and would not have hesitated with Peter to have said, " Though all men deny thee, yet will not I; I am ready to go with thee to prison and to death."

Alas! how is the much fine gold become dim, and how are the spiritual weapons of my warfare perished; thy dead men were not slain in battle, Oh, Lucifer, son of the morning, fallen how low, from highest rapture to desponding woe.

I was charged by Mr. H. L. to exhort in public, and though, as I have stated, I believed it to be the will of

God, yet it was a cross I never would reconcile myself to, nor have I ever admitted my name to be on a plan as a local preacher, at any time. I began to cry "the burden of the Lord," and the wolf of hell insinuated to me, that it was a mere chimera,—an infatuation of the brain, to think of sins forgiven;—prayer began to sit silent on my lips, and my devotional fervor gradually died away; closet duty was neglected, the substance of the means was lost in the latter, and my spiritual energies grew lifeless.

There is a gradation both in vice and virtue, but give way to the former in the least degree, and how soon, like Aaron's rod, will it erase every pious feeling, and swallow the last struggling remains of expiring virtue; no wonder that I then took to myself seven spirits more wicked than myself, and launched out into the excesses which I afterwards ran into. I thought, like Jonah, to run from the presence of the Lord, when I went on board a man of war, but even in those haunts of wickedness a guilty conscience followed me; I often strove to cast serious reflections from me, but they returned with double force.

I ran on in a course of sin and folly, although my way at times seemed to be hedged up—and such passages as the following have made me almost weep tears of blood. "If after having tasted the good word of life and felt the powers of the world to come," &c. "Better never to have known the way of righteousness," &c. "There remaineth therefore no more sacrifice for sin," &c. "Ye did run well," &c. "The dog hath turned again to his vomit," &c. "If the righteous man turneth away from the righteousness," &c. "Will ye also go away," &c.

Some of these or similar passages were constantly ringing in my ears, my hammock has frequently been watered with tears; and though among my shipmates I sometimes gathered my face into a smile, yet remember, "The laughing brow a troubled heart conceals." I had often read Bunyan's Pilgrim's Progress and considered myself like the apostate in the iron cage, and drew similar conclusions.

I never in my mind revolved on the blood of Christ, but the following ideas intruded themselves:—I have counted the blood of the covenant an unholy thing,—have done despite to the spirit of grace,—have crucified the Lord of Life and Glory afresh, putting him to an open shame, wounded him in the house of his friends, caused his enemies to triumph, and say, Aha, Aha, so would we have it, rase it even to the ground; I have caused the only wise and virtuous to weep in secret places. If there is joy in heaven over a sinner that repenteth, then by parity of reason, there is an infernal joy in the bottomless pit, when a Christian falls from his steadfastness. What was Paul's crimes compared to mine, when he informs us of what he did, in ignorance and unbelief—what a Manasseh, a Judas, or a Magdalen. If one sinner destroys much good, how much harm is that man calculated to do, who has been an accredited member of Christ's Church, and turns from the holy commandment delivered unto him;—where can Satan find so fit a tool; it is not uncommon for such to speak evil of the way of truth. I am thankful this was never my case.

I was once on shore at the island of Malta, and passing a hut, heard the language of prayer; I listened attentively, and found it was a soldier in the English service who had collected his family together, and they were addressing themselves to the throne of grace,—this was their regular custom twice a day.

I had forgot to mention an action I was in while in the Glory, 98; it was off Rochefort. The commander-in-chief was Sir Robert Calder, in the Prince of Wales, 98; we were second in command, having on board Rear-Admiral Stirling. The enemy consisted of 20 sail of the line, French and Spanish; our force was 15 of the line. We brought them to action about two in the afternoon, and it ceased about seven in the evening;—we had taken the Spanish ship, San Raphael, 74, and El Firm, a French 80; we continued at our quarters all night, expecting to recommence the action next morning. At daylight the drum beat to quarters, and the Admiral ordered the men to be sure every shot did execution, and not to fire at random. No signal being made, Admiral S. said, "What is Sir Robert about, why does he not engage the enemy,—make the signal ready for action?" On making this, Sir Robert inquired, by signal, what ships were ready to engage; every ship answered, "*Ready,*" except the Windsor Castle, and that ship had lost her main-mast by the board the day before; she also said, she was "*ready*," if the Admiral would order him a frigate to tow her into the line,—all was expectation and anxiety,—the men were fit to bite their fingers' ends off to be at the Frenchmen; but what was our surprise to see Sir Robert haul his wind and stand off, letting the enemy go quietly into harbour, and we were despatched to England with the prizes. Sir Robert was tried by a court martial and was severely reprimanded, but it was not long after that he was made Port Admiral at Plymouth. Had Sir John O. acted in the same manner, I believe his head's assurance would have been but frail,—but as I am more like a man that stands before the Judge, than the Judge, I shall suspend my judgment any further.

In the Glory, Barfleur, and Triumph, we had plays performed on board, and large parties of foreigners and English officers, as well as ladies and private gentlemen attended, at Lisbon, Cadiz, and Gibraltar;—I need not hint that I had a finger in the pie. In the ships just named, I introduced the singing of Psalms; for this I got the ill will of the ignorant part of the ship's companies, for if we happened to have a gale of wind within the week after, they swore the psalm-singers had brought it on.

Whenever I got on shore in England, I attended places of worship if I could. I was on shore at Plymouth, and being at the back of the singers in the gallery, they struck up the piece out of Isaiah, " Oh, thou that tellest glad tidings," &c. I could not contain, but sung lustily, having a strong bass voice; when I got into the chapel-yard, a man came to me, saying, he had listened some time, but could not think where the strange voice came from, that he found it out at last, and would be much obliged to me if I would attend their rehearsal on the Thursday following; I told him, I belonged to a man-of-war, and must be on board the next day.

I am fond of good singing in congregations, principally such tunes as they can join in; but averse to monopolizing in this part of sacred worship. I remember when this was carried to an excess in Sheffield; many instruments were brought, and choice pieces selected from Leach, Handel, &c., and at these seasons I mostly felt puffed up when singing; and perhaps, W. E. Miller was right, when he extended his arms over the singers in Norfolk-street Chapel, saying, he believed, if the grace of God was wanting in one part more than another, it was in the singing seat. Perhaps no community has so great a variety of tunes as the Methodists have, nor a better selection, the latter being attended to. Singing will have the intended effect of raising the minds and enlivening devotion, and the singers (singing with the spirit of their master, and understanding the import of what they express), will be mutually benefitted.

I was not long at Middleham before I joined the society, but though drawn by the cords of love, and sometimes feeling a measure of divine peace, yet I never had a second revelation of the love of God in pardoning me as I had before. Sometimes I have thought the reason lay here—in the former instance, I was simple and honest before God, and received the truth in the love thereof; in the latter, I had read much. I had compared Paley's Evidences, Fletcher's Appeal, and many other Christian writers, with Payne, Voltaire, Carlisle, and other infidels of the day. The Rev. John Reynolds once lent me " Locke on the *Human Understanding.*" I took notice of a passage where he says, " some men are afraid to read a book on any tenets, save their own, lest they should be converted to their principles." I thought this should not be my case, for I would take the advice of St. Paul, in the literal sense of the words, " Try all things, hold fast that which is good." I did so, till I got wise above what was written, and fancied I knew more than my teachers; possessing more logic than ten men that could render a reason. It had been infinitely better for me if I had taken his advice in another place, " As ye have received Christ so walk in him, and be not carried about with every wind of doctrine."

I remained in society, perhaps, four or five years, but felt no spiritual growth, my worldly circumstances improved, leanness of teeth was lost sight of, and though occasionally called upon to supply the place of travelling preachers, in case of indisposition or emergency, I was frequently overcome by an enemy within; and though the darling evil was known only to God and myself, yet in public speaking, how has the enemy harrassed me on this ground, frequently allowing me to mount the rostrum, before he commenced his attacks. In reading the life of Colonel Gardiner, he says, "I thought it was impossible that the grace of God could reach my case, unless he gave me a new nature." I drew the same conclusion. In reading Nelson's Journal, he prayed to be delivered from the *Great Offence,* and that God would bless him with an helpmate indeed; his prayer was heard and answered. I have ever, to the present, enjoyed what some call a *single blessedness,* but I am decidedly of opinion in this, I have missed my way,—being naturally volatile and of an easy disposition, my company has been courted, and having no *stay* at my own home, I have courted society; thus I have been led to lengths of vanity, from which, in another case, I should have been freed.

I wish you to know the man altogether, and not to suppose I am what I am not. I attend the public means at the Chapel, but have not been a member of society for upwards of three years, my reasons for leaving were as follows:—In the time of harvest I had been out with a friend to a harvest field, and as is customary here, visitors do (or ought) to give a trifle to the laborious and sun burnt harvesters; this I and my friend did, and we drank with them till I was at least three sheets in the wind, or half seas over; conscious of my fault, the next morning I sent my ticket to the preacher, saying, I considered myself no longer a member of society; that if I could not be a credit I was determined not to be a disgrace to them. The lines written in poetry, beginning with these words, " Friends, should you feel," &c. were written on observing the Christian friends repair to chapel on the Sunday after my revolt, and are characteristic of my feelings at that time. The piece beginning with, " Chanticleer's voice," &c. I placed over my fire-place. " Esau repentance sought," &c. was written when bordering on despair. " Brown's wish," when tempted strongly to disbelieve the Scriptures. After all, I am out of hell, what a mercy! —after all, his spirit strives—love unspeakable ; he has not yet said spirit strive no more with him ; Ephraim is joined to his idols, let him alone. He has not said, let him that is filthy, remain filthy still ;—let him that is unjust, remain unjust still ;—cut him down, why cumbereth he the ground? I sometimes think, were I restored to the favor of God, I should surely, like Bunyan's Christian, put my fingers in my ears, crying out, " Eternal life, eternal life."

I conclude with a word to such as do stand.— Christian, thou standest by faith, boast not, " thou bearest not the root, but the root thee ;" " Let him that standeth, take heed lest he fall ;" "Let not him that putteth on the armour rejoice, as he that putteth it off." I call upon thee, Christian, whatever sect, party, or denomination thou mayest form a part of, for I am persuaded when the Christian man or woman gets to heaven, then there will be no enquiring, art thou, or wast thou, a churchman, methodist, ranter, quaker, or what not :—No ; thy name shall be penitent sinner, persevering believer, final overcomer.

"Dost thou desire to know or see,
What thy mysterious name shall be,
Contending for thy native home,
Thy final foe in death o'ercome;
Till then, thou searchest out in vain,
What nought but conquest can explain."

I say, I call upon thee to give all diligence that thou mayest make thy calling and election sure; that thou so run, as finally to obtain the prize and lay hold on eternal life, adding to thy faith, virtue, temperance, patience, meekness, charity, and all the gifts and graces of the Divine Spirit;—keep thine heart with all diligence;—let no root of bitterness springing up trouble thee;—let thy spiritual life be hid with Christ in God, live in him, to him, and for him;—let every word, thought, and act of thy life, be such as thy master may approve;—live in peace, and the God of peace shall be with thee:—pursuing this line of conduct, thou shalt grow up into Christ thy living head in all things, and finally be presented before God and his holy angels without spot and blameless, thou shalt come to thy grave in a good age, and when closing thy earthly career, hear a voice say, *Come up hither—well done.*— But in following the advice offered, thou hast been seeking thine own. Know then, there are other imperious duties devolve upon thee, and it is at the peril of thy soul thou neglect them: esteem them that labour in the word and doctrine very highly, for their work's sake; while it is their duty to watch over your souls as those that must give account,—giving a word in season, bringing forth out of the sacred treasury of God's word things new and old, rightly dividing the word of truth; remember it is yours, to help them by your prayers, to add to their spiritual energies by seeing you stand fast in the Lord, and by every proper means to assist them in promoting the Redeemer's kingdom among men. Remember the words of him whom you profess to love, "Another commandment give I unto you, that ye *love one another;*"—drive to its native hell, all backsliding, whispering, slandering, and tale-bearing; ye that are strong, see that ye bear with the *casual* infirmities of the weak; work and work together, strive and strive together, ardently contending for the faith once delivered to the saints. And if stronger souls forsake the faith, let them serve as beacons to thee, and listen to the master's voice, "What is that to thee, follow thou me." If thou canst neither prevent their falling away, nor succeed in bringing the wanderer back, thou standest by faith—be not high-minded, but fear; but it is thine to recover from the wolf of hell, a sheep that has strayed out of the fold of Christ. How is this to be effected? wilt thou upbraid him for his folly? Not so, my brother. Wilt thou treat him with coolness and indifference? Oh, do not this folly. Has thy brother fallen among thieves, and wilt thou pass by on the other side? Has Satan succeeded in tripping up his heels, cast him into the mire of sin, and endeavours to throw him into the slough of despond. Is this an immortal spirit for which Christ died; and wilt thou, Oh, man of God, be an idle spectator? Wilt thou not rather weep between the porch and the altar? Wilt thou not stretch every nerve, by thy ghostly counsel, thy affectionate regard, to endeavour to bring such an one back to the Christian Church? If thou art a Christian, I am persuaded thou wilt do this and much more. "Brethren, if any among you be overtaken in a fault, ye which are spiritual, restore such an one in the spirit of meekness, considering thyself, lest thou be also tempted." Remember the strength of the Church consists in unity; if thou succeedest in bringing back one, it makes the difference of two,—the enemy loses one, and thou hast gained one. Well, but you say, instances are not wanting, where a person has fallen perhaps seven times, and ought we to attempt his recovery. I ask thee, has he fallen seventy times seven, if so, thou shalt forgive him, I suppose thou hast recovered a backslider, and upon his restoration he becomes a burning and a shining light, and finishes his course triumphing in the faith of Jesus. Wouldst thou object to him as thy crown of rejoicing in the day of God? I trow not; "What thine hand findeth to do then, do it with thy might." Strengthen the weak hands, confirm the wavering, visit the fatherless children and the widow, and all that are desolate and oppressed in mind, body, or estate; point the dying to a risen Saviour; in every part of your deportment let your light shine, and see to it, that ye adorn the doctrine of God our Saviour in all things.

I conclude my address to thee, Christian, by saying, " Brethren, the time is short." This is the time for sowing the seed, if thou sowest sparingly, or if thou sowest bountifully, thou also shalt reap bountifully or sparingly ; the seed thou now sowest will have its fruit in eternity, mayest thou so sow as to secure in the present life an hundred fold, and in the world to come, life everlasting. But how shall a *backslider* address a *backslider?* I feel somewhat at a loss ; I answer, I would have no one to come, nor those to remain in the same condemnation. When I address thee, I address myself, come then, let us reason together.

Q. Are the consolations of God small with thee? Is there no secret thing, no Dalilah, no darling lust, no idol ?

A. Yes, there is ; and this entwines itself round the heart, like ivy round the oak ; nay, it is as it were interwoven in my very nature, and seems a part of myself.

Q. But is any thing too hard for the Lord ?

A. I once thought not ; but my evil nature returned, after I thought I had clean escaped the pollutions that are in the world through lust.

Q. When thou didst feel thy evil nature so returning, didst thou cry mightily to God for help, in this thy time of need ?

A. It were well had I done so ; instead of which I parleyed with the evil, and was presently carried away by the current.

Q. Did not the spirit of God strive with thee as

did with Beersheba's devotee David, when he beheld her washing herself?

A. Yes, let God be just when he appeareth, I felt, but cursed lust, having conceived, brought forth sin, and sin brought spiritual death into my soul.

Q. And art thou still a willing captive, or art thou desirous to be freed?

A. My soul lies in ruins, and I see no way of escape! —wretched man that I am, who shall deliver me.

Q. Hast thou never heard of a specific for thy malady, I can assure thee there is such a thing, and it is called *Balm,* and may be had in Gilead?

A. Too well I know ; it was the very medicine that perfected my cure previous to my relapse.

Q. Thou hadst better go again, he will be better to thee than a stranger, for he knows thy case.

A. I dare not, for I have not attended to the prescriptions he gave me, and I shall incur his displeasure.

Q. Thou wilt indeed incur his displeasure if thou dost not speedily return, and it is not easy to endure his wrath if it be kindled but a little ; beside, though thou hast destroyed thyself, there is no other name given among men whereby thou canst be healed ;—he giveth to all men liberally and upbraideth not.

A. I would fain arise and go to him, but am so weak and wounded, and the place so far off, I am afraid I should never reach it.

Q. I am aware of thy great distance from the physician, but he has a way by the which thou mayst be brought nigh, the words have gone from his lips,—

peace to them that are nigh, and peace to them that are afar off. I perceive the nature of thy disorder, and for thy comfort tell thee, however inveterate thy case, he that gave himself for the healing of the nations will heal thee, having healed thousands.

A. I feel greatly encouraged, and am determined to make the attempt; I will arise and acknowledge my transgression and my sin,—Lord help me.

Q. Dost thou not behold him running to embrace thee with the kisses of his love?

A. Yes, it is my much offended father, and he is willing to restore me to inward health, Father, I have sinned, "stop, my son, bring forth the best robe"—against heaven,—"put a ring on his hand"—and in thy sight,—"and shoes on his feet"—and am no more worthy—"kill the fatted calf"—to be called thy son,—"and let us eat and be merry,"—make me as one of thy hired servants. For this my son was dead, and is alive; he was lost, and is found.

Would to God this Gospel method of reasoning would induce and encourage thy return, whosoever thou art, that knowest from whence thou art fallen. Wilt thou not return to thy first husband? was it not better with thee than it is now? Is not the Father inviting thee, return, Oh, backsliding Ephraim, I will heal thy backslidings and love thee freely. Oh, Ephraim, Ephraim, how shall I give thee up. At thy return Angels will rejoice, at thy return the Church will rejoice, and thy heart also shall dance for joy.

I have frequently laboured under a mistake in one

particular, I have been foolishly led to suppose, that because I had lost the power of godliness, the Church was sinking; whereas on the contrary, I have proved it to be rising in graces and number, and I am convinced it will do, for it is the hand of the Lord that can bring mighty things to pass. To him every knee shall bow, and every tongue confess to God.

I have witnessed many accidents and sudden deaths in my voyages at sea: I will just note two or three. When on board the Glory, 98, off Cadiz, Michael Daley, a boy, went into the mizen chains to catch a bird that had taken shelter there, being blown off the land; the boy fell overboard; Huggins, a seaman, jumped overboard to save him, he got hold with one hand and swam under the ship's stern with him. Our jolly boat was hoisted up astern, several officers had jumped into her with a view to save the two; however, the man at the fore-mast tackle let her go with a run, and the other holding on, the boat's stern split both the skull of the man and boy, and they sunk to rise no more, closely embracing each other. By the boat upsetting, the officers and men were precipitated into the sea, and it was with the utmost difficulty, Mr. Craddock, master, and some others were saved.

About the same time one of our line of battle ships had taken a Spanish prize, and had her in tow. At night in wearing she ran her down, having fifteen of her own men on board of her. Being next ship a-head, and hearing their shrieks and cries, we attempted to lower one of the quarter boats, on doing which, Mr. Hoare, (chief master's mate,) and two seamen were drowned, it blowing a gale of wind; they together with the prize were buried in the deep.—Charles Wyat fell from the main-top-mast head, his brains were dashed out by striking his head against the shot rack round the main coombings.—Samuel Taylor, second captain of the main-top, when off Marseilles, fell, or rather sprang, from the main-top-gallant yard-arm, and was no more seen,—there was something awful in his death.

The men were ordered in a sudden squall to hand top-gallant sails, the sail was clewed up, but filled with wind, and flew abaft the yard, the men could not lay out, when S. T., with oaths and imprecations, sprang from the cross-trees over their heads, thinking to catch the lift; he failed in this, and met a premature death.

A poor fellow newly volunteered, who had been a post-chaise driver, was made a sweeper on board, and not giving his grog to J. M., boatswain's mate, as many did to save themselves from startings, &c. he was what sailors call, down upon him; he had used him very ill one day, and on coming down into the birth, observing him to weep bitterly, I asked him what was the matter, he said, his heart was broke;—he was missing half an hour afterwards, and being on the high seas, must have jumped overboard.

The same infamous boatswain's mate,* had been in the constant practise of beating a poor fellow, his name was *Gordon, scavenger.* One day wanting some dirt

---

* The man who met the awful death he merited at Naples.

taking up, and having piped for the scavenger to no purpose, he went in search of him, and found him sitting in the galley with his back against the copper; without speaking he began on him with his rope's end, but the man not offering to speak or move, he found out he was dead.—Thomas Williams, a native of Ireland, had offended the officer of the watch, the latter beat him cruelly on the quarter deck, knocked him down and jumped upon his breast; the man, said, " What am I to do, sir, I will do any thing you bid me." " D—n your eyes, jump overboard, sir." " I will, sir," was the reply,"—the man ran aft, jumped into the sea, but was picked up by the Captain's orders.

The next is a short account of the death of Mr. L. boatswain; he had been suspended from duty for some time by our Captain, merely on account of his age and infirmities, and for some days confined to his cabin from illness, and I was informed he was dead. I went to his cabin, but found him alive; he asked me how I did;— he then asked me, whether I was a Catholic or a Protestant; I told him the latter; he said he was glad to hear it. I suspected by the enquiry, he wished religious consolation; I asked, if I should get the Common Prayer Book and read to him; he said, if you please. I opened at the visitation of the sick, and coming to that part where the visitor is enjoined to put the following question, " Do you forgive all men as you hope for forgiveness?" he said, there was one he had not, nor never would forgive. I asked him, whether it was the Captain; he said, No, it was neither sailor nor soldier.

I urged the necessity of dying in charity with all men; he said, " No, never, never," adding, " I say no more." He then gave three hideous yawns and expired. " Let me die the death of the righteous, and let my last end be like his."

I now conclude with a word of advice and caution.

First, To Captains in the Royal Navy.—Never leave liberty tickets signed and not filled up, in the care, or at the disposal of clerks, &c. There have been cases where men going on shore, on liberty, have been furnished with the above, and perhaps given from one to five pounds for them; on getting on shore they have filled them up, allowing two months leave of absence, &c. I need not add, desertion has been the consequence.

Secondly, I would recommend Midshipmen to keep their journals up regularly themselves. I knew a Mr. Atkins who had three years' pay to receive, and depended upon a seamen, who always told him his journal *was up to the day;* but the day previous to the Commissioners coming on board to pay the ship's company, the man informed him he had lost it overboard at sea on his passage home; he was, of course, nonsuited. I made shift to patch him up one, taking care the first and last dates were right, which was all the Commissioner looked at and he got his pay. A day's work, in which, was as follows :—Light winds and variable—employed occasionally. Nor was there more than six months of this kind altogether.

Thirdly, Let Warrant Officers *actually expend* what they set down in their monthly accounts. Had this been attended to, my old shipmate, Mr. R. would not, for a coil of rope, have served seven years in a hulk at Portsmouth.

Fourthly, All Stewards should be careful to mix a proper proportion of water and rum, and not by putting a gallon of the former extra, save for themselves a gallon of the latter. And let not Quarter-Masters, &c. connive at this, in order to come in snacks afterwards.

Fifth and lastly, Let the Surgeons administer to the men in need, the *valuable* as well as the trifling medicines with which their chests are furnished; by this means there will be little to send on shore or to return into store.

That these hints may have their desired effect on all concerned, and prove of use to the British Navy, is the sincere wish of the Author.

Middleham, August 1828.

Subscribers' Names.

Mr W. Swales,	*Middleham*
Mr R. Johnson,	*Ditto*
Mr John Ridley,	*Ditto*
Mr L. Spence,	*Ditto*
Mr Digby Collinson,	*Ditto*
Mr R. Morton,	*Ditto*
Mr Joseph Handley, jun.	*Ditto*
Mr R. Metcalf,	*Ditto*
Mr John Burton,	*Ditto*
Mr Wm. Scurrah,	*Ditto*
Mr John Thorpe,	*Ditto*
Mr George Thorpe,	*Ditto*
Mr Francis Horner,	*Ditto*
Mr Matthew Clarkson,	*Ditto*
Mr James Prest,	*Ditto*
Mr John Christian,	*Ditto,* 2 copies
Mr James Croft,	*Ditto*
Mr William Simpson,	*Ditto*
Mr John Calvert,	*Ditto*
Mr James Hutchinson,	*Ditto*
Mr Stephen Sturdy, sen.	*Ditto*
Mr Peter Buck,	*Ditto*
Mr Enos Hutchinson,	*Ditto*
Mr George Oates,	*Ashgill*
Mr G. E. Dinsdale,	*Middleham*
Mr John Mudd,	*Ditto*
Mr John Fisher,	*Ditto*
Mr R. Warrior,	*Ditto*
Rev. John Cockcroft,	*Ditto*
Mr Wm. Jebb Gill,	*Ditto*
Mr John Morgan, jun.	*Ditto*
Mr Robert Bowe,	*Ditto*

Mr Matthew Bearpark, Middleham
Mr Stephen Jones, Ditto
Mr Thomas Blaydes, Ditto
Mr William Metcalf, Ditto
Mr Jackson, Studdah
Mr Charles Lister, Middleham
Mr William Winn, Ditto
Mr Francis Croft, Ditto
Mr Thomas Shields, Ditto
Mr Darnell, Ditto
Mr Smith, Ditto
Mr Lye, Ditto
Mr Peirse, Ditto
Mr Shepherd, Ditto
Mr Cooper, Ditto
Mr Britch, Ditto
Mr Cartwright, Ditto
Mr Robert Morgan, Ditto
Mr Stephen Sturdy, jun. Ditto
Mr John Wright, jun. Ditto
Mr James Hornby, Ditto
Mr John Lupton, Ditto
Mr James Varo, Ditto
Mr Simon Place, Ditto
Mr Thomas Arnold, Ditto
Mr John Barker, Ditto
Mr Sewell, Ditto
Mr Stabler Smith, Ditto
Mr Leonard Digby, Ditto
Mr John Ashton, Ditto
Mr Peter Phillips, Ripon, 50 copies
Mr Stephen Smith, Ditto
Mr C. Downes, Ditto
Mr James Metcalf, North Stainley, 2 copies
Mr Robert Johnson, Rider
Mr Christ. Bucktin, sen. Ditto
Mr Brian Kaye, East Wilton
Mr Moses Towler, Ditto
Mr Illingworth, 2 copies
Mr William Davill,

Mr William Buck,	*Aysgarth*
Mr Leonard Holmes,	*Leyburn*
Mr James King,	*Kilgram*
Mr William Wells,	*Leyburn*
Mr George Robinson,	*Bellerby*
Mr Dennis Buckle,	*Leyburn*
Mr Mason,	2 copies
Mr Thomas Calvert,	*Bellerby*, 2 copies
Mr John Pearson,	*Agglethorpe*
Mr William Hawkins,	*Hoodswell*
Mr James Clarkson,	*Watlas*
Mr James Webster,	*West Burton*
Mr John Dixon,	*Barden*
Mr John Croft,	*Middleham*
Mr M. Peacock,	*Harnley*
Mr John Ward,	*Downham*
Mr Walton Alderson	
Thomas Edmundson, Esq.	
George Edmundson, Esq.	
Mr John Dixon,	*East Witton*
Mr William Plews,	*Leyburn*
Mr Robert Davison,	*Hornby*
Mr Dent,	*Leyburn*
Mr Anthony Wood,	*Hornby*
Mr William Butterfield,	*Leyburn*
Mr Mason,	*Hill Top*
Mr C. Bulmer,	*Bellerby*
Mr Edward Plant,	*Ditto*
Mr Joseph Singleton,	*Ditto*
Mr William Hudson,	*Hornby*
Mr James Simpson,	*Ditto*
Mr Richard Coultman,	*Leyburn*, 2 copies
Mr William Richardson,	*Spenithorne*
Mr James Carter,	*Ditto*
Mr Robert Unwin,	*Reeth*
Mr Richard Patterson,	
Mr Thomas Sedgwick,	*West Witton*
Mr John Gales,	*Ditto*
Mr William Jackson,	*Ditto*
Mr George Reynold,	*Ditto*

Mr William Lonsdale,	2 copies
Mr Richard Williamson,	*East Witton*
Mr Francis Dennison,	*Thornton*
Mr Thomas Cuthbert,	*Near Ditto*
Mr Atkinson,	*Leyburn*
Mr Thomas Rix,	*Middleham*
Mr J. A. Storey,	*Darlington*
Mr Milburne,	*Danby*
Dr. Braithwaite,	*Ditto*
Mr Benjamin Hind,	*Middleham*
Mr Thos. March Lamb,	*Ditto*
Mr William Handley,	*Ditto*
Mr Coulson,	
Mr Tallentire,	
Mr A. Fraser,	
Rev. ——. Jones,	*East Witton*
Mr Howson,	*Leyburn*
Mr James Sedgwick,	*Coverham*
Mr Joseph Calvert,	*Crakehall*
Mr William Ellis,	*Cover Bridge*
Mr John Dent,	*Mariforth*
——————,	*Elm Ings*
Mr William Tomlinson,	*West Witton*
Mr Ralph Tomlinson,	*Ditto*
Mr R. Metcalf,	
Mr R. Geldart,	*West Witton*
Mr W. Tomlin,	*Ditto*
Mr John Jackson,	*Ditto*
Mr Thomas Serjeantson,	2 copies
Mr John Tatham,	
Mr John Smith,	*West Witton*
Mr John Mark,	*Ditto*
Mr Thomas Topham,	*Ditto*
Mr John Bell,	*Wensley*
Mr Thomas Clarkson,	*Ditto*
Mr C. Scott,	*Ditto*
Mr Henry Kitchen,	*Ditto*
Mr Thomas Spence,	*Ditto*
Mr Richard Willis,	*Ditto*
Mr Humphries,	*Ditto*

Mr G. P. Custabodie,	*Wensley*
Mr Hugh Custabodie,	*Ditto*
Mr Emerson Bowes,	*Leyburn*
Mr James Johnson,	*Wensley*
Mr Leonard Umpleby,	*Melmerby*
Mr John Rundel,	*Ditto*
Mr James Taylor,	*Ditto*
Mr A. Buckle,	*Carlton*
Mr Metcalfe,	*Ditto*
Mr James Metcalfe,	
Mr R. Harrison,	*Agglethorpe*
Mr William Robinson,	*Coverham Lane*
Mr John Hoyle,	*Ditto*
Mr Watson Lonsdale,	*Ditto*
Mr Samuel Bates,	*Middleham*
Mr John Lee,	*Jerveaux Abbey*
Mr Merrington,	*Hunton*
James Ewbank, Esq.	4 copies
Mr Ralph Hawxwell,	
J. B—, Esq.	2 copies
Mr William Rayne,	2 copies
Miss Agnes Carborrell,	
Mr Richard Bruere,	
Mr Raymond Bruere,	
Mr Leonard,	*Middleham*
Mr George Collah,	*Ditto*, 3 copies
Mr T. Walker,	*Horse House*
Mr Leonard Hornby,	*Newstead*
Mr William Bendeloe,	
Mr Thomas Thompson,	*Cotsgrove*
Mr James Raper,	*Harnley*
Mr John Whaley,	*Leyburn*
Mr Francis Hutchinson,	*Ditto*
Rev. William Wyvill,	*Spenithorne*
Mr Thomas Bearpark,	*Constable Burton*
Mr Thomas Atkinson,	*Catterick-Bridge*
Mr Scroope,	2 copies
Miss Frances Scroope,	ditto
Mr G. I. Auston,	ditto
Mr R. Tomkinson,	ditto

Mr J. Smallpage,	*East Witton*
Mr W. Magan,	*Middleham*
Mr Richardson,	*Bedale*
Mr Mark Hall,	2 copies
Mr Joseph Towler,	*Masham*
Mr J. Dennison,	*Harnley*
Mr E. Carter,	*Fingall*
Mr T. Law,	*Thornton*
Mr Day,	*Thornton Stewart*
Mr Wm. Wrigley,	*Leyburn*
Mr T. Andew,	*Thornton*
Mr George Atkinson,	*Thornton Lodge*
Mr Wm. Jaques,	*Fingall*
Rev. E. Wyvill,	*Ditto*
Mr Stephen Kilburne,	*Ditto*
Mr Nathan Heslop,	*Constable Burton*
Mr C. Wallock,	*Ditto*
Mr Spence,	*Middleham*
Mr Abraham Smedley,	*Constable Burton*
Mr Ralph Hood,	*Ditto*
M. Wyvill, Esq. M. P.	*Ditto*
Mr Richard Ellingworth,	*Ditto*
Mr Isaac Wood,	*Ditto*
Mr Robinson Gregory,	*Catterick-Bridge*
Mr C. Scott,	*Ditto*
Mr Moses,	*Stoop House*
Mr H. T. Robinson,	*Hedgeley*
Mr Hammond,	*West Burton*
Rev. E. R. O.	*Coverham*
Mr Robert Lister	*Ditto*
Mr Kendray,	*Hammerton*
Mr Fryer,	*Marske*
Mr Thomas Hamilton,	*Ditto*
Mr William Taylor,	*Ditto*
Mr Mason,	*Bainbridge*
Mr O. Walker,	*Hawes*
Mr Dinsdale,	*Askrig*
Mr Joseph Ryder,	*Redmire*
Mr James Cooper	*Grinton*
Mr Robert Sunter,	*Carperby Green*

Mr William Wright,	*Watlas*
Mr Jaques,	*Fingall*
Mr John Blythe,	*Hawes*
Mr John Armler,	
Mr James Cloughton,	*Bedale*
Mr Fothergill,	*Leyburn*
Mr Morley Braithwaite,	*Hawes*
Mr John Deacon,	*Reeth,* 2 copies
Mr William Metcalfe,	*Ditto,* 2 copies
Mr Bowes,	*Ditto,* 2 copies
Mr Thomas Smith,	*Ditto*
Mr Joseph Longstaff,	*Ditto*
Mr Joseph M'Collah,	*Ditto,* 4 copies
Mr John Wilkinson,	*Ditto*
Mr C. Croft,	*Ditto*
Mr John Houthet,	*Marske*
Mr George Coates,	*Reeth*
Mr Thomas Ward,	*Ditto*
Mr John Burley,	*Marske*
Mr Douthwaite,	2 copies
Mr Robert Hutchinson,	*Reeth*
Mr Thomas Coates,	*Ditto*
Mr Nathan Rucroft,	*Ditto*
Mr John Robinson,	*Ditto*
Mr John Bradberry,	
Mr John Stubbs,	
Mr Thomas Coates,	
Mr Barker,	*Healaugh*
Mr George Wilson,	*Ditto*
Mr George Swallwell,	*Ditto*
Mr Ralph Gill,	*Feetham*
Mr Lodge,	*Askrigg*
Mr Edward Thomson,	*Ditto*
Mr William Metcalf,	
Mr Bowman,	2 copies
Mr Peter Storey,	
Rev. S. L. Brougham,	*Askrigg*
Mr Richard Balderston,	*Ditto*
Mr Edward Thompson,	*Ditto*
Mr Edward Waisthall,	*Ditto*

Mr Anth. Wharton, jun.	
Mr James Scarr,	*Bainbridge*
Mr L. Metcalfe,	*Hawes*
Mr George Bowes,	*Ditto*
Mr George Tempest,	*Ditto*
Mr William Lister,	*Ditto*
Mr James Cunnion,	*Ditto*
Mr Joseph Seddle,	*Ditto*
Henry Chapman,	*Thornton*
Mr Richard Wine,	*Worton*
Mr John Terry,	*Askrigg*
Mr William Coates,	*Thoralby*
Mr Thomas Metcalf,	*Worton*
Mr John Scarr Foster,	*Bainbridge*
Mr Coulton,	*Hawes*
Mr John Metcalfe,	
Mr John Garth,	*Aysgarth*
Mr John Weay,	*Ditto*
Rev. ——. Winn,	*Ditto*
Mr Joseph Shields,	*Bolton*
Mr Phillip Bennison,	*Thousby*
Mr James Horseman,	
Mr Hutchinson Wood,	*Redmire*
Mr Tobias Craddock,	*Ditto*
Mr Anthony Craddock,	*Ditto*
Mr John Wensby,	*Ditto*
Mr Wm. Robinson, sen.	*Ditto*
Mr Matthew Whitelock,	*Jerveaux Abbey*
Mr Giles Scott,	*Bellerby*
Mr Joseph Ryder,	*Ditto*
Lupton Topham, Esq.	
Thomas Robinson, Esq.	

THE END.

York: Printed by T. Weightman.